NINTH HOUR

Bishop K.D. Collins

CONTENTS

EXPLANATIONS

Abbreviations from Genesis to Revelations:

Some short books are not abbreviated

Gen.	Genesis
Ex.	Exodus
Lev.	Leviticus
Num.	Numbers
Deut.	Deuteronomy
Josh.	Joshua
Judg.	Judges
Ruth	Ruth
1Sam.	1Samuels
2Sam.	2Samuels
1Chr.	1Chronicles
2Chr.	2Chronicles
1Kgs.	1Kings
2Kgs.	2Kings
Ezra	Ezra
Neh.	Nehemiah

Est.	Esther
Job	Job
Ps.	Psalms
Prv.	Proverbs
Eccl.	Ecclesiastes
Sol.	Solomon
Is.	Isaiah
Jer.	Jeremiah
Lam.	Lamentations
Ezek.	Ezekiel
Dan.	Daniel
Hos.	Hosea
Joel	Joel
Amos	Amos
Obad.	Obadiah
Jon.	Jonah
Mic.	Micah
Nah.	Nahum
Hab.	Habakkuk
Zeph.	Zephaniah
Hag.	Haggai
Zech.	Zechariah
Mal.	Malachi
Mat.	Matthew
Mark	Mark
Luke	Luke
Jhn.	John
Acts	Acts
Rom.	Romans
1Cor.	1Corinthians
2Cor.	2Corinthians

Gal.   Galatians
Eph.   Ephesians
Phil.   Philippians
Col.   Colossians
1Ths.   1Thessalonians
2Ths.   2Thessalonians
1Tim.   1Timothy
2Tim.   2Timothy
Tit.   Titus
Phil.   Philemon
Heb.   Hebrews
Jam.   James
1Pet.   1Peter
2Pet.   2Peter
1Jhn.   1John
2Jhn.   2John
3Jhn.   3John
Jude   Jude
Rev.   Revelation

Scriptural points

Instead of explanations and commentary, many Scriptures have been used to bear out certain points. This is because the author believes in surrendering to the Scriptures where the point is clear enough in the Scriptures and a little fear of over-simplification. All Scriptures are taken from the King James Version unless otherwise noted.

FOREWARD

'*N*inth Hour' *is a book that everyone needs to read as a timely reminder that we are living in the closing chapters of history. Drawing upon the metaphor of the ninth hour in the Old Testament as the hour that God demands nothing but sacrifice and repentance Dr. Collins draws a parallel to the urgency of our times. Throughout the times in Scripture particularly during the Old Testament era God positions people as seers and prophets to remind us not to get too comfortable but to watch the times and seasons. I believe Bishop Collins carries this prophetic mandate for our time and this book is pregnant with prophetic insight. This book is a wakeup call to churches and world leaders and all people as to the time that we are living in. In this timely book Bishop Collins takes us through a detailed analysis and exegesis of prophecies encoded in the sacred text of Holy Scripture. Utilizing the analytical and exegetical tools of mathematical formulae and scientific deduction the author decodes and exposes*

profound and troubling truths pertinent to world history today.

The Ninth Hour is a treasure loaded with information and prophetic pronouncements that reminds us that the Bible is a current book that speaks to every situation that the world is facing today. After reading this book readers will never read the Bible the same way again as it is frightening how current and 'dreadful' the Word of God is. Using the Ninth Hour revelations Bishops Collins unfolds many layers of frightening truths about the current state of world affairs from the recent USA election to the economic meltdown.

To sleeping church leaders slumbering on the ease of prosperity preaching to people with itching ears this book is a wakeup call to return to the prophetic mandate and prepare people for the second coming. To world leaders and politicians the Ninth Hour is a warning of the coming judgment when the God of heaven will bring in a new world order. To the sinner the Ninth Hour is a call to repentance because the time is at hand. To the backslider the Ninth Hour is a call to return to their first love. To believers who await the coming of our Lord Jesus Christ, the Ninth Hour is a sign to remain prayerful and faithful because your redemption draws near.

Bishop Dr. Keith Collins the Presiding Bishop of the Harvest Army Church International is a rear leader with uncompromising standards and an independent spirit unmoved by the trends of these times. This book is not just the product of his intellectual propensity but one that is birth through prayer and fasting as Dr Collins is a man of deep devotion and spiritual discipline.

Over the years he has poured into my life and I am grateful to him and his wife Rev. Mrs. Collins and the Harvest Army Family worldwide for their love and support.

Rev. Dr. Clifton Clarke PhD
Regent University
Professor of Missions and World Christianity
Ordained Bishop New Testament Church of God (Cleveland TN)
Director and Founder of West Afrika Ministries

PREFACE

*A*s I rush to get this book completed I realize how important it is to get it into the hands of every saint and sinner. I may not be the most qualified theologically to do this book, however I had no choice after that unusual visitation on July 24, 2004. On that uneventful morning I heard the firm riveting voice say 'Nine' at 8:37 AM.

Instantly I began to preach about it in many churches and indeed on international television. This was followed up by the astounding frequency of the number in world moving events.

It is important to note that the ninth hour in this context is not depicted as a particular hour, day, week, month or year but a season of dramatic fulfillment of the revelation. The scripture says 'And he changeth times and seasons..... Daniel 2:22. Though we have seen astounding drama leading into year 2009, the revelation is referring to a **season, how long, I know not. It could be years or even decades.**

This does not mean that particular years to even hours in real time may not be shown as having a preponderance of fulfillment. For example another prophecy noted on www.harvestarmy.org, predicted that 2007 – 2009 would be particular years of judgment from God.

By the time of the writing of this book, it was already common knowledge that 2007 was the most scandalous year in the Body of Christ in a century. Hundreds and possibly thousands of Ministries and Ministers, great and small had fallen into disgrace. Judgment began in God's house.

2008 made history as the most devastating economic collapse on the earth since nearly a century. By January 2009, the first black President of the USA was already inaugurated, maybe the first in the world of any country of white majority. The following month February 2009 registered over 663,000 jobs lost in that month alone and nearly 6,000,000 in a year.

By this time the entire country of Iceland had already collapsed economically; The continent of Asia had spiraled into economic chaos; Europe accompanied the USA with financial bail outs in trillions of US dollars to no avail. Some countries actually closed their stock market at different times.

Equally, crime and terrorism had escalated to levels causing political anxiety worldwide. Strangely, by April 2009 even real piracy had emerged as a multi-million dollar industry on the coasts of Africa taking at least one American ship among more than 100.

On Sunday April 5, 2009 the sermon preached at our mid-day 'City Son Service' in New York was the *'NINTH HOUR'*. *Over 500 people were in attendance. It was streamed live worldwide on the internet at Streamingfaith.com. By **9:32** PM(EDT) the same day earthquake struck Italy. It was **6.3** on the Richter's scale; It was **8.8** Kilometers deep.*

*Concerning the time 9:32 PM, the **9**[th] hour is clearly the period between 9 and 10 (AM or PM). Concerning 6.3 on the Richter's scale, 6 + 3 = **9**. Because of the parameters in seismological measurement 8.8 KM is easily rounded as **9KM***

I must thank my wife Rev. Euphema Collins for her continued encouragement to write this book. She followed up at every moment noting its urgency. I must also thank Evangelist Shamesha Mckoy and her husband Minister Kirk Mckoy for their detailed work in editing the manuscript. Evangelist Tenika Bailey has done splendidly in coordinating the relevant submissions.

My prayer is that this book will resurrect and renew the sensitivity we need to the voice of God as He speaks to us of His plans for mankind then fulfill it before our eyes.

*Dedicated to all true Prophets of God who stand for
righteousness, holiness, integrity and humility.*

WHAT TIME IS IT?

God's purpose for man and His mandate upon the Body of Christ are among the most popular subjects in Christendom. They are heralded in many books even to the level of college credit. Several great servants of God including, Rick Warren and Miles Munroe, have published books on these very important subjects. The main ingredient, however, has not been fully explored. This vital ingredient is the matter of the 'time'.

God's purpose for man cannot be fully recognized without sufficient attention to the aspect of **time**. This time is referring to all kinds including: time of day, day of the week, month of the year, year date, decade, century, millennium, seasons, periods, ages, dispensations. It also includes times in terms of happenings, events and any variable that helps the on-looker to identify a particular point in time or a period. For example, the times of the Gentiles refers to the time since Christ to the Rapture.

The scripture says "a wise man's heart discerneth both **time** and judgment because to every **purpose** there is **time** and judgment, therefore the misery of man is upon him. For he knoweth not that which shall be: for who can tell him **when** it shall be?" (Eccl. 8:5 – 7)

Discerning the time is so important in God's purpose for man that he declares a person who fails to do so a hypocrite (Luke 12:56).

God also declares wiser than some people, the stork, the crane and the swallow who observe the time of their coming. He then asks, "How do ye say, We are wise?" He then raps it up by declaring where to look to discern the time 'The wise men are ashamed, they are dismayed and taken: lo they have rejected the word of the Lord and what wisdom is in them'(Jeremiah 8:7-9).

Now check this out. It is already hypocritical, unwise and detrimental to not know the time. Then it becomes more challenging when we hear that God actually changes the times.

Dan.2:21 - "And he changeth the times and the seasons: he removeth kings, and setteth up kings: he giveth wisdom unto the wise, and knowledge to them that know understanding."

In dealing with Israel, knowledge of the times was paramount. Specially gifted people were appointed to pay attention to that aspect of their lives (1Chron 12:32)

Many scriptures point to the ways God intend for us to discern the time. This includes visions, dreams and other gifts of the Spirit (Ezek.12:27; Dan.2:9; 8:17; 10:1; Hab.2:3)

A RIVETING VOICE

ANGEL OF GOD'S VOICE: On Saturday morning **July 24, 2004**, my face was on my pillow on the right side of my bed. Without turning around to look physically, I saw a vague figure of the Angel of the Lord standing on the left corner of the bed foot, behind me. The Lord pointed to me and said in a firm, low, riveting tone '**Nine**' (He said nothing else). I opened my eyes and looked at the clock which said (**8:37**) '**23 Minutes to 9**'. This was a confirmation of the revelation. Note also that 8 + 3 + 7 = 18; 1 + 8 = **9**

My wife awoke and I immediately told her about it. We jumped out of the bed and ran downstairs to see the news for anything unusual. There was nothing spectacular on the news. Nevertheless my wife and I remained troubled about this vision.

The following day July 25, 2004 I was booked to speak at the Annual State Convention of Calvary Church of God in Brooklyn, New York. I imparted the vision of the number '**Nine**' to them and warned of the **'Countdown to the Showdown'** between good and evil, upon the earth.

By the same evening of July 25, 2004, our Church Administrator showed me a rebate check in the amount of **$ 9,300** (after a recent purchase of a church building). This was in the midst of a back breaking need of the church. This was another confirmation.

It was then discovered shortly after, that **'The Great Gathering'**, a major international event, hosted by our church, was already advertised in the media to begin on **August 8, 2004.** This worked out to be **23 days** to the **9th month** (September). (Remember that **'23 Minutes to 9'** was the time I looked at the clock). Of course September has **'9'** letters. September 2004 the year I saw this revelation began on a **'Wednesday'** the only day of the week with **'9'** letters.

By Monday July 26, 2004 the news reported of **electrical transformer(s)** blown up mysteriously in Manhattan at roughly **9 AM**. Several blocks shut down.

The revelation was subsequently spoken in as many avenues of publicity as would open their doors. These included several churches, media programs and of course our nearly ten years running prophecy page on our web site www.harvestarmy.org.

Fast-forward to January 2007 when this Book was initially being penned. A refugee church in Ghana, West Africa that we had never heard of declared **'72'** days of fasting and prayer for the Harvest Army Ministry. This was slated to begin on January **'18'**, **2008.** One cannot help but notice that these numbers

(72: 7+2 = **'9'** & 18: 1+8 = **'9'**) coincide directly with the vision.

Ladies and gentlemen, the tides have changed. The tables have turned. The clock is heralding: *It is the "Ninth Hour"*.

As time went on and still goes on, God continued and continues to confirm this vision of the "Ninth Hour". You will discover this to be a riveting repetition throughout this pulsating revelation of this Hour. The confirmations are extremely overwhelming.

SPIRITUAL BLINDNESS

No one credibly prophesied of the terrorist attacks of September 11, 2001. By credibility I mean not only with sufficient precision but that the messenger utilized optimum effort to get it published worldwide **before** the event took place. Of course, after the event, hundreds of embarrassed prophets and prophetesses tried to hint at some awareness but it was powerless without being judged (1Cor. 14:29) and unfortunately it helped no one.

No one credibly prophesied of the devastation of New Orleans by "Hurricane Katrina". Of course, audio, video and even written prophecies were unearthed **after** the fact. Some seemed quite impressive but lacked the aspect of publicity before.

Even a true prophecy that can be proven to be received before the event is of no use but for the promotion of the speaker if it is unearthed only after the event. To dig up an accurately recorded version of the prophecy is still not totally prophetic. The power in the prophecy is the risk taken by the prophesying person **before** the event, the scrutiny it undergoes and the benefits gained because of advance knowledge. This is what separates false religion from Christianity: "And now I have told you before it come to pass, that when it is come to pass, ye might **believe me**." John 14:29

Many years ago it was a mystery why many pregnant women died during child's birth. In later years it was discovered that they died because of ignorance of the work of micro-organism on and in the body. As the eyes of scientists and doctors were opened, with the use of microscopic devices, they were able to stop most of these deaths and indeed many others. As in the physical, this scenario is true in the spiritual. Spiritual death is the order of the day even in the midst of the best theologians and established clergy. As Christians, we need to develop our spiritual microscope and be brave and honest about our findings. We should crave to see the micro-organisms so much that it causes us to wash our senses (hands, eyes, ears, mouth, nostrils) every time they get soiled, and actually every time possible.

As the world and even the church degenerate in major calamities of 60% divorce, perpetual adultery and homosexuality from the clergy and much more, many so-called "good people" who have screamed 'legalism' and 'religion' for every scriptural guideline will discover their only way of survival is microscopic insight (spiritual sight). It is the disregard for many of these guidelines that have blunted the gift of prophecy, discerning of spirits and interpretation from arising to our rescue.

We behave foolishly. How do we expect to hear much from the Lord prophetically when we disregard the revelations of his written microscope (The Holy Bible)? It is called "a more sure Word of prophecy" (2 Peter 1:19). The Scripture goes on to say 'The wise men are ashamed, they are taken: lo, they have rejected the word of the Lord and what wisdom is in them?" Jer 8:9)

Now, after fully utilizing the already existing spiritual microscope of the Holy Bible, God promises to show us "great and mighty things which we know not of" (Jer 33:3). As a matter of fact he has already shown us "new things from this time even hidden things and we know not of them" (Isaiah 48:6)

It is when we walk according to God's words that this prevailing spiritual blindness will dissipate

NINTH HOUR
OF WHAT ?

JUDGMENT

This is the dreaded, most pronounced and dramatic part of the "Ninth Hour". It is the most prevalent part that no one wants to acknowledge or declare. Judgment however, does not automatically mean trouble. It basically means "justice" as is rightly interpreted from many Scripture passages with the word "judgment".

Believers in Christ have nothing to fear as the Scripture declares that God will not destroy the righteous with the wicked. Another scripture says "...... Behold I send evil upon all flesh, saith the Lord: but thy life will I give you as a prey in all places whither thou goest"(Jer. 45:5).

On another score, even if the righteous dies physically with the wicked it will just be a change of their state of existence on earth as the righteous is immediately translated into a heavenly state yet remaining the same person. The wicked obviously translates into a hellish state experiencing further tragedy, torment and damnation forever.

Take note of the following Scripture: Is 42:14, "I have long time holden my peace; I have been still, and refrained myself: now will I cry like a travailing woman; I will destroy and devour at once."

The travail of women regularly takes **nine (9)** Months. Now, look at the following aspects of the "Ninth Hour" being an hour of God's judgment.

The word 'gematria' has to do with the code within the numbering system of the Biblical languages. By these numberings, certain conclusions and even prophecies can be realized and understood. Many Biblical numerologists have made the following conclusions about the number nine; (the specifics of E.W. Bullinger in his book 'Number in Scripture' are astounding):

* Gematria of **'My Wrath'** is **999**
* Gematria of **'Dan'** is **54 (9x6)**, which mean judge.
* Gematria of **'Verily, Verily'** is **99** means summing up and ending
* In Genesis 19:4-29, the gematria of the judgments upon **Sodom** amounts to multiples of nine (**9**) (89550 = 9 x 9950).
* Nine(**9**) judgments are recorded for the stingy believer in Haggai1:11 (Land, Mountains, Corn, New Wine, Oil, That which the ground bringeth forth, Men, Cattle, Labor)

*   Nine(**9**) original words exist for Judgment: **(9)** Dikee, dikaios, dikaioo, dikaiosunee, dikaios, dikaioma, dikaiosis, dikasttees, dikaiokristrisia.

Words related to Judgment appear **nine times** in the Bible
- Abussos: bottomless pit, deep
- Asebees: ungodly
- Aselgeia: lasciviousness
- Astrapee: lightning

Factor of 666 **(9x74)** - Judgment of the Anti-Christ (spirit, system & beast)

9 is Related to 6: Six(6) is the sum of its factors **(3x3=9) (3+3=6).** This could signify the end of an era of man.

9 INVERTED_(Satanist inverts everything of God for eg; Cross inverted). Six(6) is the number for man and Six,Six,Six(666) is the number for Satan, the Antichrist and the False Prophet) 666 divides perfectly by 9.

The **"Ninth Hour"** of this dispensation, the hour of finality and judgment, probably began on **September 11, 2001**. Here are the alibis:
- September: **9** letters
- Terrorism: **9** letters
- Manhattan **9** letters
- Time of attack was roughly **9** AM (between (8:48 & 9:10)

- 8:48 - 9:10 = 22 Minutes: the total time of the attack between both towers = 11 minutes each. (**9.11**)
- The number 11 means disorder, <u>disintegration</u>
- The number 9 divides perfectly into 666 the dreaded number (9 x 74 = 666). 7 + 4 = 11

I did not realize the dramatic occurrence of the number 9 until after my revelation experience on July 24, 2004. 2004 was also interesting as the ninth month began on a Wednesday(9 letters).

Mathew 27:46 And about the **"Ninth Hour"** Jesus cried with a loud voice, saying, Eli, Eli, lama sabach-thani? That is to say, my God, my God, why hast thou forsaken me."
:51 And behold the veil of the temple was rent in twain from the top to the bottom and the earth did **quake** and the rocks rent.

Jhn 5:27 And hath given him authority to execute **judgment** also because he is the son of man.

Acts 17:30 And the times of this ignorance God winked at, but now commandeth all men everywhere to repent.
:31 Because he hath appointed a day, in the which he will **judge** the world in righteousness by that man whom he hath ordained..........

The "Ninth Hour" represents the end of the grace dispensation. The sum of the 22 letters of the Hebrew Alphabet is 4995 *(5x999)*. The number five(5) is believed to represent 'Grace'. Therefore this period is stamped with grace and finality, fitting before **judgment**.

SACRIFICE

This season of Judgment will demand much sacrifice from God's people. The ""Ninth Hour"" was the hour of temple sacrifice unto God. In this hour God will be moved by nothing less than sacrifice.

Believers will have to demonstrate to Him that they willingly want what He offers. We will not be able to blame God like Adam did, telling Him that He was at fault for giving him Eve. God demonstrated and exemplified this sacrificial requirement in this hour, by the ultimate sacrifice of death on the cross. 'And about the **"Ninth Hour"** Jesus **cried** with a loud voice, saying, Eli, Eli, lama sabachthani? That is to say, my God, my God, why hast thou forsaken me'. Mth 27:46

PRAYER

The ""Ninth Hour"" also involved the importance of prayer during this season. This was also the actual hour of prayer daily. It was a major time of the day when the very incense burnt in the temple could be smelled from 50 miles away. Some commentators even say the women barely wore perfumes at that time. This emphasizes the level of effect that the times of prayer should have upon the society; "....the effectual fervent prayer of a righteous man availeth much Jam.5:16

REVELATION

Of course how could we be blind in this season when God promises to reveal the major things to his servants the prophets (Amos.3:7). The "Ninth Hour" is the hour of revelation. It is the hour of great understanding of many puzzles of the past. It is evident in many scriptures including Joel 2:28 which speaks of dreams, visions and all saints prophesying.

It is interesting to discover that the word 'eighteen' (18) appears in order in the word 'enlightenment'. The numerical digits add to 9 (1 + 8 = 9). "For with thee is the fountain of life. In thy light we see light "Ps.36:9

Ezra 9:8 And now for a little space grace hath been shown from the Lord our God, to leave us a remnant to escape, and to give us a nail in his holy place, that our God may **lighten our eyes** and give us a little reviving in our bondage

FULFILLMENT

For many decades, skeptics jeered at the Christians for the many prophecies found in the Bible which seemed weird and impossible. In this hour they will be overrun by the continual unquestionable fulfillment of prophecy. Their only recourse will be to repent and believe the gospel or rise up to persecute the people of the Gospel.

The number nine (**9**), being the last of the single numbers, means finality, not necessarily the end of the world, but the final chapter of the Dispensation of Grace or the church. It can therefore be understood as the time of fulfillment, judgment, examination, confrontation, the showdown, conclusion, exposure, totality, fullness, revelation, outpouring, reckoning, harvest, maximization, reward, etc.

The Scripture declares that a time of fulfillment of God's prophecies would become evident on the earth. Every believer must strive to emulate the pulse of this season.

Matthew 24:3 And as he sat upon the mount of Olives, the disciples came unto him privately, saying, tell us, **when** shall these things be ? and what shall be the **sign** of thy coming, and of the end of the age.

:4 And Jesus answered and said unto them, take heed that no man deceive you.

:5 For many shall come in my name, saying, I am Christ and shall deceive many.

:6 And ye shall hear of **wars and rumors of wars:** see that ye be not troubled: for all these things must come to pass, but the end is not yet.

:7 for nation shall rise against nation, and kingdom against kingdom: and there shall be **famines** and **pestilences** and **earthquakes** in divers places

:8 All these are the beginning of sorrows

:9 Then shall they deliver you up to be **afflicted,** and shall **kill you:** and ye shall be **hated** of all nations for my name's sake.

:10 And then shall many be **offended,** and shall **betray** one another and shall hate one another.

:11 And many **false prophets** shall rise, and shall deceive many.

:12 And because iniquity shall abound, the love of many shall wax **cold.**

:13 But he that shall endure to the end, the same shall be saved.

:14 And this **Gospel** of the Kingdom shall be **preached** in all the world for a witness unto all nations; and then shall the end come.

Mth 24:34 Verily I say unto you, This generation shall not pass, till all **these things** be **fulfilled**.

:35 Heaven and earth shall pass away but my words shall not pass away

Jhn13:18 I speak not of you all: I know whom I have chosen: but that the Scripture may be **fulfilled**, he that eateth bread with me hath lifted up his heel against me.

:19 Now I **tell you before** it come, that, when it is **come to pass**, ye may believe that I am he.

Jhn 16:4 But these things have **I told you** that when **the time** shall come, ye may remember that **I told you** of them

Jhn 14;29 And now I have **told you before** it come to pass, that, when it is **come to pass**, ye might believe me.

Eph 1:10 That in the dispensation of the **fullness of times** he might gather together in one **all things** in

Christ both which are in heaven and which are on the earth even in him: In whom we have obtained an inheritance, being predestinated according to the purpose of him who worketh all things after the counsel of his own will.

Lk.21:22 For these be the days of vengeance that all things that are **written** may be **fulfilled**

:24 And they shall fall by the edge of the sword, and shall be led away captive into all nations: and Jerusalem shall be trodden down of the gentiles, until the **times of the Gentiles be fulfilled.**

In this 'Ninth Hour', God will fulfill His words.

HARVEST

This is the hour when more souls will be born than the church has seen for a long time. It is depicted by the **'nine months'** that a woman takes to bear a child. A woman is a type of the church. Like the time of Noah, it is the time of the great end-time harvest during great judgment and before the Second Coming of Christ.

2Kings 4: 16 And he said, about this **season** according to the time of **life**, thou shalt embrace a son. And she said, nay, my Lord, thou man of God, do not lie unto thine handmaid

:17 And the woman conceived, and bare a son at the **season** that Elisha had said unto her, according to the time of **life**

41

HOLINESS

In this hour, God is demanding holiness than ever before.. Ungodly living will be met with God's wrath. Jeremiah.23:20 says, "The anger of the Lord shall not return, until he have executed, and he have performed the thoughts of his heart: in the latter days ye shall consider it perfectly." Isaiah 26:9 states "… With my soul have I desired thee in the night; yea, with my spirit within me will I seek thee early: for when thy judgments are in the earth, the inhabitants of the world will learn righteousness.

Holy Ghost (**9** letters)

Fruit of The Spirit: (**9**)

Love, Joy, peace, longsuffering, gentleness, goodness, faith, meekness, temperance. Galatians 5:22

Beatitude (**9** letters), (**9** beatitudes)

Poor in spirit, mourn, meek, righteous, merciful, pure, peacemakers, persecuted, manner of evil. Matthews 5:3-12

SHOWDOWN

Today, many have been presumptuous enough to challenge the veracity of God and his people. Like the events of Elijah on Mount Carmel, the atheists, agnostics and all skeptics will be greatly ashamed. The time of the evening sacrifice when Elijah challenged the prophets of Baal was the ""Ninth Hour"".

1Kings.18:36 And it came to pass at the time of the offering of the **evening sacrifice**("Ninth Hour") that Elijah the prophet came near, and said, Lord God of Abraham, Isaac and of Israel, let it be known this day that **thou art God** in Israel, and that **I am thy servant**, and that I have done all these things at thy word.

:38 hear me, O Lord, hear me, that this people may **know** that thou art **the Lord God**, and that thou hast turned their heart back again.

:39 And the fire of the lord fell and consumed the burnt sacrifice and the wood, and the stones, and the dust, and licked up the water that was in the trench.

:39 And when all the people saw it, they fell on their faces: and they said, **The Lord he is the God**: the Lord he is the God.

Of course we will not want to order the scourging and physical deaths of the mockers of God. Moreover, this would be a present day crime. God himself will order it even to the displeasure of some of his saints. 'Behold ye despisers, and wonder and perish: for I work a work in your days, a work which ye shall in no wise believe though a man declare it unto you. Acts' 13:41.

The 'showdown' between good and evil will mark the unprecedented time we live in: "The "Ninth Hour"".

RECOGNITION

This is the hour of recognition and reward when God will conspicuously bless the hard work of his faithful followers worldwide. Many believers who have never been heard of will burst on the scene as their prayers will be answered and their blessing will become evident to the whole world.

<u>Acts 10:3</u> He saw a vision evidently about the **"Ninth Hour"** of the day an Angel of God coming to him, and saying unto him, **Cornelius** (9 letters).

:4 And when he looked on him, he was afraid, and said, What is this, lord? And he said unto him, **thy prayers** and thine alms are come up for a **memorial before God**.

MIRACLES

Shortly after the first outpouring in Jerusalem, on the Day of Pentecost, the disciples experienced and performed miracles that shook the norms of medicine and science of those times.

<u>Acts. 3:1</u> Now Peter and John went up together into the temple at the hour of **prayer** being the **"Ninth Hour"**.

:2 And a certain man lame from his mother's womb was carried, whom they laid daily at the gate of the temple which is called Beautiful, to ask alms of them that entered into the temple.

:6 Then Peter said, Silver and gold have I none; but such as I have give I thee; In the name of Jesus Christ of Nazareth rise up and walk.

:10 And they knew that it was he which sat for alms at the Beautiful gate of the temple: and they were filled with wonder and amazement at that which had happened unto him.

This time it will be much greater than those days. It will be similar to the abundance of the "Latter Rain" in a physical sense.

In the midst of persecution, and much calamity, creative miracles will abound like the world has never seen. They will undoubtedly come from the Lord, free from divination and witchcraft.

Though much prayer and fasting will precede these miracles, it will not be hindered from the church as it is the time. Many will be saved, but many will be hardened against God nevertheless.

ABUNDANCE

In the midst of the judgment of the ninth hour, the Scripture tells us to bring our donation in store to God's House. This, spent on spreading the Covenant (The Gospel), will cause abundance. (Deuteronomy 8:18).

Lev.25:22 And ye shall sow the eighth year, and eat yet of old fruit until the **ninth year**; until her fruits come in ye shall eat of the old store.

PRESIDENT BARACK OBAMA

Look at the following prophecy extrapolated from the prophecy page of harvestarmy.org. *'July 24, 2004 God has revealed the number NINE (9) as the Prophetic Number for the last of the last days. (The interpretation of this is that the countdown to the showdown' between good and evil has began. This number will be evident in many FUTURE HAPPENINGS'*

Up to a month before the historic USA presidential elections of November 2008, I had no idea who would win until a woman of God reminded me of the "Ninth Hour" revelation. I compared the names of the contenders and considered that Barack Obama would win. By this time however even the worst election pundits had figured that he would win anyway

- The word **'President'** has **9** letters.
- His full name **'Barack Hussein Obama'** has 18 letters (1 + 8 = **9**)

- From the very date and night of the **'Dream Speech'** (August 28, 1963) of the great civil right leader Rev. Dr. Martin Luther King Jr. to the **'Nomination Acceptance Speech'** of Barack Obama (August 28, 2008), was **45** years on the exact date and even the night. (4 + 5 = **9**)
- President elect Barack Obama had his first press conference after his election victory with 17 senior advisors plus himself. 17 + 1 = 18. (1 + 8 = **9**)
- He was inaugurated on January 20, 200**9**
- He inherited the worst financial crisis in modern history, which began in September 2008. '**SEPTEMBER**' has **9** letters
- During the presidential election, the electorate in California USA voted against homosexual marriages and put in question 18,000 of them in the state. 1 + 8 + 0 + 0 = **9**
- By November 2008 while he was still President – Elect several countries in Europe had already gone into '**RECESSION**' – **9** letters.

As early as September 27, 2005 the following prophecy was published on harvestarmy.org :

*"New pages are being turned on the earth. A **NEW CHAPTER** is about to unfold on the earth. What is unknown will not prevent the dramatic **CHANGES**. They will be rapid*

and will have the drama of a new season or a sub-dispensation".

Take note that the overshadowing theme of his campaign and rise to power was **CHANGE** .

God had already prophesied of a plot to bring down the USA by several means including political isolation. (See prophecy page of harvestarmy.org).

Nov. 25, 07 **'A PLOT TO BRING DOWN AMERICA'** *is afoot. It involves several aspects including: Humanitarian Indictment, Energy Blockade, Nuclear Siege, Sexual Suicide, Christian Incarceration, Riches Criminalized,* **POLITICAL ISOLATION,** *Media Murder,* **'FINANCIAL SUBSTITUTION',** *Legal intimidation, Ecological Criminalization, Terrorism.*

The above does not necessarily mean that President Barack Obama will be a bad President. He will, however, be a historical time marker of an era of the judgment of God on mankind.

President Obama will preside over the most powerful country in the world at a time when the world is descending into unprecedented poverty, chaos and retribution. He will lead the USA during the consequential emergence of a new chapter on the earth, a new world order with a severely weakened USA.

By November 2008 the news had reported that the President of Russia had already met with European Leaders to begin the enactment of a New World Order in opposition to the USA

(Telegraph.co.uk Oct. 8, 2008 by Adrian Bloomfield, picture by Associated Press)

By January 5, 2009 former Secretary of State Henry Kissinger had named Barack Obama the leader of a new world order. His first formal interview after his inauguration as President was on January 27, 2009. This was to a Saudi Arabian television station 'Alarabira'(9 letters). It may seem insignificant but the frequency of the nine letters here should be noted

From Bible times God would mark time by the ascent or descent of Kings and great leaders; for example, "In the year that King Uzziah died..." (Isaiah 6:1).

One of the underrated aspects of Barack Obama's rise to world power is God's Providence. God promised that racial integration would be an important aspect of his providence and hence, could not be stopped. This is one of the main areas missed by Politicians who are resistant to immigration and racial integration. If they do not acknowledge this and change their policies they will hardly ever win again.

"And hath made of one blood all nations of men for to dwell on all the face of the earth, and hath determined the times before appointed, and the bounds of their habitation" Acts.17:26

It was God's providential protection of Israel that Moses be married to an Ethiopian woman. Like many politicians and media moguls today, Moses' brother and sister criticized him privately. God judged them severely for this. Esther, a Jewish lady married to a Gentile king to ensure the safety of the Jewish nation.

"After this I beheld and lo a *great multitude* which no man could number of all nations and kindreds and people and tongues, stood before the lamb, clothed with white robes and palms in their hand " (Rev.7:9).

God even providentially anointed Cyrus, a heathen king, for the protection of his providential people (Isaiah 45).

President Barack Obama's rise to power will significantly affect changes which will reflect the pulsation of this hour, the "Ninth Hour".

It is important to note that his use of the theme 'change' is not unique to him: During this period other historical changes were impossible to ignore especially in the USA. Some of the political aspects include the following:

- Nancy Pelosi was recently serving as the first female Speaker of the House of Representatives in the USA government (3rd in line of presidency)
- Hillary Clinton, a woman, nearly won the nomination for the Democrat Party.
- Sarah Palin of Alaska , a woman, contended for Vice President as a Republican.
- John McCain would have become the oldest President in USA History if he had won.
- January 30, 2009 Michael Steele a black man was voted the Chairman of the Republican Party by January 30, 2009
- February 2, 2009 Eric Holder, a black man was voted as Attorney General for the USA.
- In other countries:

- February 1, 2009 Johanna Sigurdardottir became the first female Prime Minister of Iceland.
- February 2, 2009 Muammar Abu Minyar al-Gaddafi of Libya was named head of the African Union for a year. (politically isolated worldwide for decades for alleged role in terrorism)

To write it bluntly, this is clearly the beginning a special time of worldwide political change prophesied in the Scripture. God predicted that during a time of worldwide economic collapse, political leadership would change dramatically.

Is.3:1 For, behold, the Lord, the LORD of hosts, doth take away from Jerusalem and from Judah the stay and the staff, the whole stay of bread, and the whole stay of water,

:6 When a man shall take hold of his brother of the house of his father, saying, Thou hast clothing, be thou our ruler, and let this ruin be under thy hand

:7 In that day shall he swear, saying, I will not be an healer; for in my house is neither bread nor clothing: make me not a ruler of the people.

However such fulfillment would need a whole book so stay abreast.

FULFILLMENT BEGINS

NO PAST WORLD EVENTS

The number nine(**9**) seems to be negligible in occurrence from the greater world events in the recent past. It therefore points mainly to the **future.**

Absent from World War (**1914**)
Absent from World War II (**1941**)
Absent from the birth of the nation of Israel
    (**1948**)
Absent from Israel's capture of Jerusalem
    (**1967**)
Absent from Martin Luther King's death (**1968**)
Absent from President J.F. Kennedy's death
    (**1968**)
Absent from the fall of the Soviet Union (**1988**)

As said before, the September 11 attack is the only previous event that rivals the September 2004 designation. The number nine (9) is strongly evident in this (designation).

September 11, 2001

September 11, 2001 could be the sign of the emergence or unfolding of the "Ninth Hour". Up to that date terrorism was not yet a common word except for the suicide - homicide bombings in Israel.

Airplanes used as missiles, bombed the World Trade Center, in Manhattan, New York City, leaving thousands dead. A third plane slammed into the Pentagon Building in Washington killing hundreds. A fourth plane was yanked from the terrorist by brave passengers and crashed as they headed for the White House.

The formidability of September 11, 2001 as the emerging date is borne out by the following facts:

- Nearly 3,000 dead. The most people ever dying in a terrorist attack up to that date.
- The most damage to the world economy since the great depression of the 1930's
- Triggered at least two wars that have dramatically affected the world
- Dramatically affected immigration policies and travel worldwide
- Dramatically changed the matter of security in all aspects of the society worldwide

The number nine shows significant occurrence in the following areas:

Terrorism	9 Letters
September	9th Month
September	9 Letters
Time	9 AM (8:48 & 9:10)
Manhattan	9 letters
90 Minutes:	The time it took for the towers to fall after the first strike

1.8 million tons of materials and debris were reported to have been removed from the site

September 2003
A heat wave hit France, where the staging of the September Eleven took place. It left 15,000 dead

September   9 letters

December 26, 2003
Earthquake hit Iran, the largest sponsor of terrorism worldwide. It left 35,000 dead

Terrorism   9 letters.

March 11. 2004

Terrorism bombings struck the rail system in *Spain*. It left 198 dead.

Terrorism   9 letters

July 7, 2004

Terrorist bombed the railroad system in London. It left 56 dead.

Terrorism   9 Letters

Date   July seven, two thousand and four. 27 letters; $2 + 7 = 9$

Time   9 Minutes to 9

September 2004

The occurrence of the number nine has been much more prevalent since September 2004 and can in some ways rival September 11. 2001.

'September': (9 letters)

'Wednesday': (9 letters) 1st day of September 2004

'Two Thousand and Four': (18 letters) $(1+8 = 9)$

'September, Two Thousand and Four': (27 letters: $2+7 = 9$)

Hurricanes hit the Caribbean causing floods of historical proportion. It left 3,000 dead.

Hurricane: (9 letters)
- Strongest season in history then
- Reported to be the most expensive cost for reconstruction in history ($18 Billion in history. 1+8 = 9).
- Strangely, Hurricane *Ivan* made a U-turn and returned to Florida, went west to Gulf of Mexico and hit USA again in Texas.
- Hurricane *Jeanne* followed, went out to sea after passing Bahamas, made a U-turn and hit Florida at the same spot as Hurricane *Francis* and followed the same path.

Caribbean (9 letters): where hurricanes started. This area also received the most of the damage. Hurricane is believed to mean 'evil god of the Caribbean'

Gulf Coast (9 letters): Region where it landed

Pensacola (9 letters): City worst hit by *Ivan* in USA. More than 50 dead. The latest storm damage in Pensacola had happened in 1995, nine (**9**) years before 2004.

During the same period of 2004 it was impossible to ignore the repeated occurrence of the number nine in the purported Dan Rather - CBS document blunder against the then President of the USA George W. Bush. Look at this allegation:

Deception:	9 letters
News Media	9 letters
Dan Rather	9 letters [Main news Anchor]
Mary Mapes	9 letters [Main producer]
John Kerry ?	9 letters [This document blunder was rumored to be an attempt by some to help his presidency, though not proven]
Tom Brokaw	(9 letters) of NBC seemingly defended Dan Rather

'News Memos' (9 letters) allegedly sent by ABC telling their staff journalist not to treat President Bush equally as Senator Kerry

Earthquake: 6.0 at Parkfield (9 letters), California, strongest since 1966

Rejection: (9 letters) (September 21) Majority of the nations of the world snubbed the USA President at United Nations. No ovation for first time in history.

Terrorism (9 letters) Worst Massacre in Russia. 400 dead, 600 wounded

December 26, 2004

Earthquake in the ocean caused tsunami of historical proportions to hit several countries. The main country hit by far Indonesia estimated at over 230,000 dead

Indonesia	9 letters, maximum death
Earthquake	9. on Richter scale
South Asia	9 letters
Banda Aceh	9 letters, first place of impact
Tsunami	9 AM, struck land
Date	December 26). December 26 is exactly 117 Days after September 1, 2004. (1+1+7=9)

August - September 2005

Hurricane Katrina and Rita hit the Gulf Coast causing floods of historical proportions. It left 1,500 dead.

Hurricane	9 letters
Gulf Coast	9 letters

Louisiana   9 letters

Ninth Ward 9th Ward of New Orleans

Ninth Ward   9 letters

Abbeville   9 letters (A community
heavily hit)

A courthouse was reported to be the only major building left standing in Cameron. This could be evidence of God's judgment.

October 8, 2005
Earthquake in Pakistan left 80,000 dead.

South Asia   9 letters

Islamabad   9 letters (Main city hit)

Jalalabad   9 letters (Another city heavily
                     hit)

Himalayas   9 letters (the mountain range
                     involved)

Time   9 AM roughly

October 8, 2005
Hurricane hit Guatemala in South America. It left 1,000 dead

Hurricane   9 letters

Guatemala   9 letters

May 27, 2006
Earthquake hit Indonesia, left 6000 dead

Indonesia   9 letters

June 5, 2006
Islamic Militants capture Mogadishu, capital of Somalia, feared haven for Al-Qaeda terrorist

Mogadishu   9 letters

June 7, 2006
The world's 2nd most notorious Terrorist Al Zarqawi killed in Iraq.

Al Zarqawi: 9 letters

June 12, 2006
Reports that Al Muhajer is new leader of Al-Qaeda in Iraq.

Al Muhajer   9 letters

July 4, 2006
North Korea's longest range missile 'Taepodong discovered to be able to hit US allies, South Korea, Japan, Australia etc and USA itself. It was launched but failed after 40 seconds.

Taepodong   9 letters

July 12 - August 14, 2006
Hezbollah Terrorist in Southern Lebanon kidnap two Israelite soldiers, allegedly without provocation. Israel responds with bombings in Lebanon. Hezbollah bombs Haifa in Israel and other cities. 900 dead

Terrorism: 9 letters

Hezbollah: 9 letters

Nazrallah: 9 letters (head of Hezbollah in Lebanon)

Iran - Syria 9 letters Accused of being sponsoring the attacks.

President of Iran, Mahmoud Ahmadinejad (18 letters-can be perfectly divided by 9): the alleged main sponsor of Hezbollah

Kofi Annan (9 letters) - Allegedly accuses Israel of deliberately killing UN observers

Seize-Fire (9 letters) eventually followed after the bombings

August 31, 2006
Iran defies call by most of world community to halt nuclear weapons development.

Mahmoud Ahmadinejad (18 letters-can be perfectly divided by 9): **President** of Iran.

September 2006

In a surprise move, the US Supreme Court contemplated removal of the Ten Commandments from government buildings.

9 Justices

September	9 letters (Chief Judge Confirmed)
9th Judge:	Major battle on to fill the 9th place, but eventually confirmed.

October 9, 2006

'Pyongyang' (9 letters) Head of North Korea

November 16, 2006

Earthquake **8.1** on Richter's Scale causing tsunami (8+1=9).

December 29, 2006

King of Babylon (Saddam Hussein) executed 27 years after his reign started, since 1979.....2 + 7 = 9

January 1, 2007

Same as (1 . 1 . 07): 1 + 1 + 7 = 9

Bulgaria & Romania joined the 'European Union' bringing the total member countries to **27** countries (2 + 7 = 9).

Bulgaria & Romania were previously '**Communist**' Countries (9 letters)

Many scholars of prophecy believe that the 'European Union' is the 'Revived Roman Empire" 18 letters .....1 + 8 = 9

New Secretary General of the United Nations Chosen: 'Banki-Moon' (9 Letters)

January 15, 2007

President of Iran meets with South American Countries for alleged 'Anti-US Alliance' (IRAN - VENEZUELA - NICARAGUA - ECUADOR - BOLIVIA).

- Venezuela ......9 Letters
- Nicaragua .... 9 Letters
- 'Iran - Ecuador - Bolivia' (18 Letters) .... 1 + 8 = 9
- Iran, Venezuela, Nicaragua, Ecuador, Bolivia (36 letters) ..... 3 + 6 = 9

January 31, 2007

Venezuela's government give their President power to make National decrees for 18 months
Venezuela 9 letters
18 months 1 + 8 = 9

Socialism 9 letters (declared to be coming)

Communism 9 letters (eventually)

February 27, 2007

Largest Stock market drop in USA and world-wide since September 11, 01

- The main trigger was a dramatic drop in China's stock market of **9** %
- It happened on '2 . 27 . 07'. All digits added = 18 (1 + 8 = 9)

March 5, 2007

Earthquake in Sumatra, Indonesia:

- 6.3 in magnitude; perfectly divided by 9
- Indonesia 9 letters

May 4, 08

Cyclone(storm) in Myanmar(Burma), Up to - 134,000 Dead /

9,000 Dead in first report

900 Trapped in first report

'QINGCHUAN': 9 Letters. (Main area hit)

July 2008

Earthquake in Los Angeles:

5.4 magnitude 5 + 4 = 9

27 aftershocks 2 + 7 = 9

3.6 magnitude strongest aftershock 3 + 6 = 9

Cell Phone: (interrupted) 9 letters

September 12, 2008

Hurricane Ike brings much destruction to Texas & Louisiana
Hurricane 9 letters
Galveston (Main place hit) 9 letters
Last major hurricane in Galveston 108 years ago. $1 + 0 + 8 = 9$
Louisiana (9 letters) also hit greatly

September 15, 2008

Worst 'WALL STREET COLLAPSE' since 1929: $3,000,000,000,000 (3 trillion) lost
September (9 letters)

October 14, 2008

Russian President reportedly calls for New World Order to " isolate the USA" (Political Isolation).

November 08

Barack Obama becomes President –Elect for the USA

'Barack Hussein Obama' 18 letters $1 + 8 = 9$

MATHEMATICAL ANALYSIS

The number nine(9) is the most mind-boggling number. This is because of the hair raising uniqueness non-existent with any other number.

Last Single Number

There is no single number beyond nine. Those beyond are combinations of the first nine numbers of value

Largest Single Number

There is no single number larger than nine. Those larger are combinations of one to nine.

Value

There are only nine(9) single numbers of value by themselves (1,2,3,4,5,6,7,8,9).

Zero '0' has no value

All single numbers add to 45
(1+2+3+4+5+6+7+8+9 = 45) 4+5 = 9

Encompassing:

Mathematically speaking, the number nine '9' is encompassing. Some have called it inescapable and mysteriously invincible. It does not matter how many times you multiply it, the sum of the result will always equal 9.

No other number works this way.

9 x 2 = 18,   1 + 8 = 9

9 x 3 = 27,   2 + 7 = 9

9 x 4 = 36,   3 + 6 = 9

9 x 5 = 45,   4 + 5 = 9

9 x 6 = 54,   5 + 4 = 9

9 x 7 = 63,   6 + 3 = 9

9 x 8 = 72,   7 + 2 = 9

9 x 9 = 81,   8 + 1 = 9

9 x 10 = 90   9 + 0 = 9

You need another step to get to 9 when using 9x11, or 9x21, 9x22, 31, 41, 51 and so on; (for e.g. 9x11=99, 9+9=18; 9x21= 189, 1+8+9=18).

It is interesting that **9x11** is the first multiplication which needs a 2nd step before arriving at nine. This could represent the 2 towers of the World Trade Center on September 11, 2001

Number of planets:
Until recently it was common knowledge worldwide that the solar system has **9** planets.

2Kgs. 23:5 And he put down the idolatrous priests, whom the kings of Judah had ordained to burn incense in the high places in the cities of Judah, and in the places round about Jerusalem; them also that burned incense unto Baal, to the sun, and to the moon, and to the <u>planets,</u> and to all the host of heaven.

Geometry of the earth
The 360 degrees of the circle adds to 9, meaning "control" or "compass"

Is.40:22 It is he that sitteth upon the <u>circle</u> of the earth, and the inhabitants thereof are like grasshoppers.

Diameter of the earth
7,920 is the number of statute miles of the mean diameter of Earth.

$$7 + 9 + 2 + 0 = 18; 1 + 8 = 9$$

Prv.30:4 Who hath ascended up into heaven, or descended ? who hath gathered the wind in his fist ? who hath established all the <u>ends of the earth</u> ? what is his name, and what is his son's name, if thou canst tell.

Speed of the earth
Average speed of the earth as it orbits around the Sun is 666 Miles per hour

$$6 + 6 + 6 = 18; 1 + 8 = 9$$

Radius of the earth
From the North or South Pole to the equator is exactly 5400 nautical miles

$$5 + 4 + 0 + 0 = 9$$

Prv.30:4 Who hath ascended up into heaven, or descended ? who hath gathered the wind in his fist ? who hath established all the ends of the earth ? what is his name, and what is his son's name, if thou canst tell.

Polar circumference of the earth
21,600 nautical miles

$$2 + 1 + 6 + 0 + 0 = 9$$

Is.40:12 Who hath measured the waters in the hollow of his hand, and meted out heaven with the span

Name of God

The Hebrew 4-letter name for God is YHVH which has a gematric value of 9. We all know God is Love. 'Love' has a gematric value of 9.

God's presence

Represented by (Ark of Covenant): the cubit dimensions when converted to inches was 45 ins x 27 ins x 27 ins. This can be evenly divided by 9 (1 cubit = 18 ins)

Ex 25:10 And they shall make an ark of shittim wood: two(2) cubits and a half(1/2) - (45 ins) shall be the length thereof, and a cubit and a half (27 ins) the breadth thereof, and a cubit(1) and a half(1/2) (27 ins) the height thereof.

Refuge :

- Total life spans of the 10 patriarchs from Adam to Noah (The flood), = 1656 years

    1 + 6 + 5 + 6 = 18; 1 + 8 = 9

Noah's Ark

The Dimensions of the Noah's Ark can be perfectly divided by 9 when converted from cubits to inches: 540 ins x 900 ins x 540 ins (1 cubit = 18 ins). In addition,

    540: 5 + 4 + 0 = 9
    900: 9 + 0 + 0 = 9

Hope

New Jerusalem: 12,000 furlongs long, wide & high. If this is converted to measurement in "feet" , it equals 7,920,000 ft, equally divisible by 9. In addition,

$$7 + 9 + 2 + 0 + 0 + 0 + 0 = 18; 1 + 8 = 9$$

Rev.21:16 And the city lieth foursquare, and the length is as large as the breath; and he measured the city with the reed, <u>twelve thousand furlongs</u>. The length and the breath and the height of it are equal.

CHRISTIAN
AWE

Christian 9 letters

It is interesting that such bedrock nickname or label for the followers of Jesus Christ has nine letters. This signals completion and conclusion indicating that all other religions are actually false

Acts 11:26 ….. And the disciples were called <u>Christians</u> first at Antioch.

Acts 26:28 Then Agrippa said unto Paul, almost thou persuadest me to be a <u>Christian</u>.

1Pet 4:16 Yet if any man suffer as a <u>Christian,</u> let him not be ashamed; but let him glorify God on his behalf.

Holy Bible 9 letters

Holy Ghost 9 letters

Sacrifice 9 letters

Scripture 9 letters

Christmas 9 letters

9 gifts of the spirit according to 1st Corinthians 12:8 - 10

1Corinthians.12:8 For to one is given by the Spirit the word of <u>wisdom</u>; to another the word of <u>knowledge</u> by the same Spirit;

:9 To another <u>faith</u> by the same Spirit; to another the gifts of <u>healing</u> by the same Spirit;

:10 To another the working of <u>miracles</u>; to another <u>prophecy</u>; to another <u>discerning</u> of spirits; to another divers kinds of <u>tongues</u>; to another the <u>interpretation</u> of tongues.

1. Word of Wisdom
2. Word of Knowledge
3. Faith
4. Healing
5. Working of Miracles
6. Prophecy
7. Discerning of spirits
8. Divers kind of Tongues
9. Interpretation of Tongues

Harvester 9 Letters

A believer who reaps the harvest of souls can rightly be called a Harvester.

Matthew 9:37 Then saith he unto the disciples, The harvest is truly plenteous but the laborers are few;
:38 Pray ye therefore the Lord of the harvest, that he will send forth laborers into the harvest

Personal Evangelism (18 letters: 1 + 8 = 9)

Prayer and Fasting
Prayer and Fasting is like a woman in travail. Under normal circumstances a woman takes nine (**9**) months to travail before giving birth. God depicts his church like a woman in travail

Isaiah 66:8 Who hath heard such a thing? who hath seen such things? Shall the earth be made in a day? or shall a nation be born at once? for as soon as Zion travailed, she brought forth her children

God also depicts Himself as God in travail of his mercy towards mankind until it is expired and his wrath is birthed.
.

Isaiah 42:14 I have long time held my peace; I have been still and refrained myself: now I cry like a travailing woman; I will destroy and devour at once.

PROVIDENTIAL TIMING

Providence actually means fate. The secular world refers to it as luck. For God it means His ordered future or 'future history', things that will happen despite any intervention outside of God. He Himself will not intervene because he has ordained it to be so despite everything else. The book of Revelation is more than prophecy. Much of it is future history or providential.

God's providence is:
- Greater than the power of prayer, praise, faith, worship, promises, blessings, etc
- Not negotiable.
- Enforced by dramatic events which include Natural Disasters, Un-natural Disasters, Political Upheaval, Inventions, Discoveries, Endowments(Ps.75:6,7).
- It is not exactly the same as prophecy, neither God's Will, Predestination, Eternal Security etc. For example: It is God's will that his

people prosper and be in good health even as their soul prospereth (3John 1:2). This is conditional and therefore avoidable. God's Providence, however, is unconditional and unavoidable.

- Like an unstoppable train bearing down on an insane man who braces himself against the tracks to stop it. It is like a war tank 100 miles high. It will instantly crush or remove all
- Does not control the details of life as many teach but instead, ensure that the foundations or pillars remain unchanged.

PILLARS OF PROVIDENCE

The word

Mth.5:18 For verily I say unto you, Till heaven and earth pass , one jot or one title shall in no wise pass from the law, till all be fulfilled.

Ps.119:89 Forever, O lord, thy word is settled in heaven

Rev.22:18, 19 ...if any man shall add unto these things, God shall add unto him the plagues that are written in this book.

:19 And if any man shall take away from the words of the book of this prophecy, God shall take away his part out of the book of life and out of the holy city and from the things which are written in this book.

Ps.119:128 Therefore I esteem all thy precepts concerning all things to be right; and I hate every false way

Hell

Is.5:14 Therefore hell hath enlarged herself and opened her mouth without measure and her glory and their multitude, and their pomp, and he that rejoiceth shall descend into it.

Is.14:12 How art thou fallen from heaven O Lucifer.............
:16 They that see thee shall narrowly look upon thee, and consider thee, saying, is this the man that made the earth to tremble, that did shake kingdoms.
:19 But thou art cast out of thy grave like an abominable branch, and as the raiment of those that are slain, thrust through with a sword, that go down to the stones of the pit, as a carcass trodden under feet

Heaven

1Ths. 4:16 For the Lord himself shall descend from heaven with a shout with the voice of an archangel, and with the trump of God and the dead in Christ shall rise first.
:17 Then we which are alive and remain shall be caught together with them in the clouds to meet the Lord in the air: and so shall we ever be with the lord.

World Revival

Mth 24:14 And this gospel of the kingdom shall be preached in all the world for a witness unto all nations and them shall the end come.

Joel 2:28 And it shall come to pass afterward, that I will pour out my spirit upon all flesh; and your sons and your daughters shall prophesy, your old men shall dream dreams, your young men shall see visions:

Is.11:9 They shall not hurt nor destroy in all my holy mountain: for the earth shall be filled with the knowledge of the Lord as the waters cover the sea.

Israel

Is.45:17 But Israel shall be saved in the lord with an everlasting salvation. Ye shall not be confounded world without end.

Is 14:25 That I will break the Assyrian in my land, and upon my mountains tread him under foot: then shall his yoke depart from off them, and his burden depart from off them, and his burden depart from off their shoulders.
:26 This is the purpose that is purposed upon the whole earth: and this is the hand that is stretched out upon all the nations.
:27 For the lord of host hath purposed and who shall disannul it. and his hand is stretched out, and who shall turn it back

Reproduction

Gen.1:28 And God blessed them, and God said unto them, be fruitful, and multiply, and replenish the earth and subdue it: and have dominion over the fish of the sea, and over the fowl of the air, and over every living thing that moveth upon the earth

Racial Harmony

Acts.17:26 and hath made of *one blood* all nations of men for to dwell on all the face of the earth, and hath determined the bounds of their habitation.

Rev.7:9 After this I beheld and lo a *great multitude* which no man could number of all nations and kindreds and people and tongues, stood before the lamb, clothed with white robes and palms in their hand.

Jhn.17:20 Neither pray I for these alone, but for them also which *shall believe* on me through their word.
      :22 And the glory which thou gavest me I have given them; that they may be one even as we are one.
      :23 I in them, and thou in me, that they may be made *perfect* in one, and that the world may know that thou hast sent me, and hast loved them, as thou hast loved me.

EXAMPLES OF PROVIDENCE
God allows certain people and events to bend the world back to his providence. These include political

upheaval, natural disasters, man made disasters and more

Biblical:

Marital situations:
- Moses: Marriage to Ethiopian.
- Hosea: Marriage to a harlot.
- Ezekiel: Death of a good wife.
- Esther: Marriage to a heathen King

Strange appointments / events
- Paul: The persecutor chosen to reach Gentiles.
- Cyrus: Heathen king, anointed by God (Isaiah 45)
- Rahab: A harlot of the enemy provided refuge for spies.
- Ephraim: Younger brother chosen over Manasseh

Greatest Apostles lived a single life:
- John: Grace apostle
- Paul: Gentile apostle

Unusual events
- Noah's Flood changed the earth
- Sodom's Hell changed behavior on the earth

General
- Israel kept in the wilderness (same shoe, clothes)

- Jeremiah told by God to:
  - actually build houses in Babylon;
  - to buy piece of land though it is captured; put receipt in buried jar because they will be returning (Jer.32:6-15)
- Paul was single / Peter was married.
- Evangelist to carry script / Other times, to carry no script.
- No preparation for court / Prepare to give an answer

Non-Biblical

- USA standing up for Israel guarantees their prosperity
- NYC mountain top for world revival

Rev.3:8 I know thy works: behold I have set before thee an open door and no man can shut it, for thou hast a little strength and hast kept my word and hast not denied my name

:10 Because thou hast kept the word of my patience, I will keep thee from the hour of temptation, which shall come upon all the world, to try them that dwell on the earth.

:12 Him that overcometh will I make a pillar in the temple of my God, and he shall go no more out: and I will write upon him the name of my God and the name of the city of god, which is New Jerusalem......

PEOPLE OF PROVIDENCE

To become people of providence the following guidelines are necessary:

- Find the Pillars of Providence;
- Find the Gap left to be filled;
- Find the servants of God who are in the gap and follow them;
- Find your place in the gap;
- Find your final destination beyond the gap;
- Discern where it is at and where it is not.- a providential church;
- Discern and seize the moment when it arrives;
- Awareness of the sacrifices needed; willingness to make them;
- Know what will not get the job done despite good efforts;
- Know what is lasting versus what is temporary;
- Know what to emphasize and where to do less;
- Know the difference between people of providence and good imposters;
- Be determined to go where it is at;
- Understand the difference between being spiritually busy and providentially led ;
- Understand the purpose of the negatives as well as the positives

PLACE OF PROVIDENCE

- The mountaintop, politically and economically speaking, has world influence. Whatever happens there spreads easily
- The providential pivot - the most crucial place(s) where the impact is most dramatic. eg New York, London. etc.
- Do you live at a certain place affected by God's Providence in a negative way?
- Is your church aligned with the Pillars of Providence ?
- Is your Pastor / Prophet / Preacher aligned with the Pillars

Other areas of God's providence includes:
- Power of Providence
- Periods of Providence
- Patterns of Providence,
- Degree of Providence
- Ministers of Providence
- Etc.

DISCERNING THE TIME

The scripture use words and phrases such as: 'This Time', 'Appointed Times', 'The Time', 'High Time', 'Stay Ye Not', 'Expedient', 'Now', 'While It Is Day', ' Say not Ye There Are Four Months', 'Past', ' Perished', Ended'.

Ps.90:12 So <u>teach us</u> to number our days, that we may apply our hearts unto <u>wisdom</u>

Ps.74:9 We see not <u>our signs</u>: There is no more <u>any prophet</u>: neither is there among us any that knoweth <u>how long</u>

Rev.13:18 Here is <u>wisdom,</u> let him that hath <u>understanding</u> count the <u>number</u> of the beast: for it is the number of man; and his number is Six hundred three-score and six (666)

Jer 8:7, 8 The stork in heaven <u>knoweth</u> her appointed times and the turtle dove and the crane and the swallow

Eccl 8:5 .....A <u>wise man's </u>heart discerneth both <u>time</u> and <u>judgment</u>

In preparing ourselves to discern the time we must do the following basic things

Repent in Fasting and Prayer

Dan.9:2 In the year of his reign I Darius understood by <u>books </u>the <u>number</u> of the years, whereof the word of the Lord came to Jeremiah the prophet, that he would accomplish seventy years in the desolations of Jerusalem
:3 And I set my face unto the Lord God, to seek by <u>prayer,</u> and supplication, with <u>fasting,</u> and sackcloth, and ashes.
:4 And I prayed unto the Lord and made my <u>confessions</u>.................

Consider the Vision

Dan 9:22 And he(Gabriel) informed me, and talked with me, and said, O Daniel, I am now come forth to give thee<u> skill</u> and <u>understanding</u>.
:23 At the beginning of thy supplications the commandment came forth, and I am come to shew thee; for thou art greatly beloved: therefore understand the matter and <u>consider</u> the vision; (for e.g.)

- Nebuchadnezzar
- Joseph

Observe the Time

Jer 8:7,8 ......the crane and the swallow <u>observe</u> the time of their coming, but my people know not the judgment of the lord; How do we say, we are wise...
- Patterns
- Trends

<u>The time is indicated by the following:</u>

1. God's Providence

The following are some of the fundamentals of God's Providence: Heaven, Hell, Israel, Church, End time revival etc..

Acts 17:26 And hath made of one blood all nations of men for to dwell on all the face of the earth, and hath <u>determined the</u> <u>times</u> before appointed and the bounds of their habitation.

:31 Because he hath <u>appointed a day</u> in the which he will judge the world in righteousness by that man whom he hath ordained.

2. Clear command of scripture

Ps.119:60 I made <u>haste,</u> and delayed not to keep thy commandments.

For example, not to work for seven(7) days weekly

3. Signs

Mth 24: Wars, Famine, Pestilence, Fig tree blossom etc.

4. **Revelations** (Dream, Vision, Word of knowledge etc.)

Gen.41:32-36 ...... and God will <u>shortly </u>bring it to pass. .....look out a man discreet and wise, and set him over the land of Egypt........ and let him appoint officers over the land. ....and let them gather all the food of those good years

- Pharaoh
- Daniel
- Paul

5. **Biblical Mathematics**

Dan 9:1 In the first year of his reign I Darius the son of Ahasuerus, of the seed of the Medes, which was made king over the realm of the Chaldeans:2 In the first year of his reign I Daniel <u>understood</u> by books, the <u>number of the years</u> whereof the word of the lord came to Jeremiah the prophet that he would accomplish 70 years in the desolations of Jerusalem

6. Time of Great Wickedness

Joel 3:13 Put in the sickle for the harvest is <u>ripe,</u> come get you down for the press is <u>full</u>, the fat overflow for their wickedness is great

Eccl 8:11 Because sentence against an evil work is not executed <u>speedily,</u> therefore the heart of the sons of men is fully set in them to do evil.

Josh 10:19 <u>Stay ye not</u>, but pursue after your enemies and smite the hindmost of them. Suffer them not to enter into their cities.

Examples include the great flood of Noah after man began to cohabit with demons; Destruction of Sodom and Gomorrah resulting from homosexuality and the many plagues and death among the Egyptians for enslaving and persecuting the Israelites

7. Departure of the Righteous

Gen 19:15, 22 And when the morning arose, then the angels hastened Lot, saying, Arise, take thy wife, and thy two daughters, which are here; lest thou be consumed in the iniquity of the city. " <u>Haste</u> thee, escape thither, for I cannot do anything till thou be gone thither."
- The 'Red Sea' was closed after Israel crossed
- Moses told to move out of the way by God
- Tribulation after the saints are raptured

8. Ripe Harvest

Today we see the largest population ever on the earth – approximately 6.7 billion people

Joel.3:13 Put in the sickle for the harvest is <u>ripe</u>, come get you down for the press is <u>full</u>, the fat overflow for their wickedness is great.

9. Unfruitful circumstances

1Kg 17:7 And it came to pass after a while that the brook <u>dried up</u>, because there had been no rain in the land

 :8 And the word of the lord came unto him, saying

 :9 Arise, get thee to Zarephath which belongeth to Zidon, and dwell there: behold I have commanded a widow woman there to sustain thee.

Prv.20:29 The glory of <u>young men</u> is their strength: and the beauty of <u>old men</u> is their grey hair.

1Jhn 2:14 I have written unto you, fathers, because ye have known him [that is] from the beginning. I have written unto you, young men, because ye are strong, and the word of God abideth in you, and ye have overcome the wicked one.

In modern times many organizations went digital too late and, as a result, lost much money.

10. Patterns / Trends

Prv.10:22 The blessing of the Lord maketh <u>rich</u> and addeth <u>no sorrow</u> to it.
- 60 % Divorce today
- Divorced ministers
- Increase in poverty
- Spread of perversion
- Incrimination of the wealthy
- Global warming
- Travel
- Education Patterns
- Music

11. Dispensations

Eph.1:9 Having made known unto us the <u>mystery</u> of <u>his will</u> according to his good pleasure which he had purposed in himself.

:10 That in the dispensation of the <u>fullness of times</u> he might <u>gather</u> together in one all things in Christ both which are in heaven and which are on earth even in him: In whom also we have obtained an inheritance, being predestinated according to the purpose of him who worketh all things after the counsel of his own will.

1Cor.9:17 For if I do this thing willingly, I have a reward: but if against my will, a dispensation of <u>the gospel</u> is committed unto me.

Eph. 3:2 If ye have heard of the dispensation of the <u>grace</u> of God which is given me to you-ward:

12. State of the Church

Rev. 3:15 I know thy works that thou art neither cold or hot.

:16 So then because thou art <u>lukewarm</u> and neither cold nor hot: I will spew thee out of my mouth.

:17 Because thou sayest I am <u>rich</u> and increased in goods, and have need of nothing; and knowest not that thou <u>wretched</u> and <u>miserable</u> and <u>poor</u> and <u>blind</u> and <u>naked</u>.

HOUR OF REVIVAL

Is.57:13 ….. I dwell in a high and lofty place, with him also of a contrite spirit to <u>revive the spirit</u> of the humble.

Opposite of Revival   (Spirit of a Deep Sleep)

Is.29:10 For the Lord hath poured out upon you the spirit of <u>deep sleep</u>, and hath closed your eyes: the prophets and your rulers, the seers hath he covered.

History of Revival   (Day of Pentecost)

Ps.85:6 Wilt thou revive us <u>again</u> that thy people may rejoice
Acts 2: And the day of Pentecost was fully come
Acts 8:1

What is Revival: (All Flesh Prophesying)

Joel 2:28And it shall come to pass afterward, that I will pour out my spirit upon all flesh; and your sons and your daughters shall prophesy, your old men shall dream dreams, your young men shall see visions:

Purpose of Revival   (Optimum Salvation of mankind)

1Cor.14:24 But if all prophesy and there come in one that believeth not, or one unlearned, he is convinced of all, he is judged of all

Signs of Revival   (Salvation & Miracles)

Mrk.16:15 And he said unto them, Go ye into all the world, and preach the gospel to every creature.
    :17. And these signs shall them that believe; in my name they shall cast out devils; they shall speak with new tongues.
    :18 They shall take up serpents; and if they drink any deadly thing, it shall not hurt them; they shall lay hands on the sick, and they shall recover.

Acts 8 :4 ....Therefore they that were scattered abroad went everywhere preaching the word.

Who will lead it   (God himself)

Is.29:14 Therefore, behold, I will proceed to do a marvelous work and a wonder: for the wisdom of their wise men shall perish and the understanding of their prudent men shall be hid.

Who will receive it quickly (Spiritual Children)

Is 28:9-12 Whom shall he teach knowledge? and whom shall he make to understand doctrine, them that are weaned from the milk and drawn from the breast

Who will boycott it; (Established Church)

Acts 13:41 Behold ye despisers, wonder and perish for I do a work in your days...

Is.48:6 Thou hast heard, see all this; and will not ye declare it? I have shewed thee new things from this time, even hidden things, and thou didst not know them.

Where will it break from: (Mountain Top)

Is.2:2 And it shall come to pass in the last days that the **mountain** of the Lord's house shall be established in the top of the mountains, and shall be exalted above the hills, and all nations shall flow unto it.

:3 And many people shall go out and say come ye, let us go up to the mountain of the Lord

Is.52:7 How beautiful **upon the mountains** are the feet of him that bringeth good tidings...

How Long will it continue   (Little Space)

Ezra 9:8 And now for a little space grace hath been showed from the Lord our God, to leave us a remnant to escape and to give us a nail in his holy place, that our God may lighten our eyes and give us a little **reviving**

:9 For we were bondmen yet our God hath not forsaken us in our bondage, but hath extended mercy unto us in the sight of the kings of Persia, to give us a **reviving** to set up the house of our God......

Hindrance   (Traditions)

Mrk 7:13 Making the word of God of none effect through your **tradition**, which ye have delivered: and many such like things do ye.

When   (Now)

Hos.6:2 After two days will he revive us...

Ps. 138:7 Though I walk in the midst of trouble, thou wilt **revive** me; thou shalt stretch forth thine hand against the wrath of thine enemies, and thy right hand shall save me.

Hab3:2 O lord I heard your speech and was afraid: o Lord, **revive** thy work in the midst of the years, in the midst of the years make known; in wrath remember mercy.

Rebels against Revival: (Legion of Jezebel)

Rev.2:20 Notwithstanding I have a few things against thee, because thou sufferest the woman **Jezebel** which calleth herself a prophetess to teach and to seduce my servants to commit **fornication** and to eat things **sacrificed unto idols.**

Rod of Revival: **(Great Tribulation)**

Rev. 2:22, 23 Behold I will cast her into a bed and them that commit adultery with her into **great tribulation** except they repent of their deeds

'Written off' from Revival   (Despisers)

Acts.13:41 Despisers, wonder and perish)

Remnants for Revival   (Those who endure Persecution)

Is.19:30 And the **remnants that are escaped** of the house of Judah shall yet again take root downward, and bear fruit upward.
    :31 For out of Jerusalem shall go forth a remnant.

Fire of Revival   (Burning desire to preach)

Jer.20 I feel like fire shut up in my bones.

Stones of Revival   (Unshakeable truths)

Neh.4:2 Will they **revive** the stones out of the heaps of the rubbish which are burned?

Hos.14:7 They that dwell under his shadow shall return; that shall **revive** as the corn, and grow as the vine.

Counterfeit Revival   (False Prophets)

(Acts 19:13 Then certain of the vagabond Jews, exorcist took upon them to call over them which had evil spirits the name of Jesus, saying we adjure you by Jesus whom Paul preacheth.

    :16 And the man in whom the evil spirit was leaped on them, and overcame them, and prevailed against them, so that they fled out of that house wounded and naked.

Spectators to Revival   (Diviners)

Acts 8:9 But there was a certain man, called Simon, which beforetime in the same city used sorcery, and bewitched the people of Samaria, giving out that himself was some great one

Remnants for the Revival

Is.19:30 And the remnant that is escaped of the house of Judah shall yet again take root downward, and bear fruit upward.

:31 For out of Jerusalem shall go forth a <u>remnant,</u> and they shal<u>l **escape**</u> out of Mount Zion: the **zeal** of the Lord of host shall do this.

Is 11:15 And the Lord shall utterly destroy the tongue of the Egyptian sea; and with his mighty wind shall he shake his hand over the river, and shall smite in the seven streams, and make men go over dryshod
:16 And there shall be a **highway** for the <u>remnant</u> of his people, which shall be left, from Assyria; like as it was to Israel in the day that he came up out of the land of Egypt.

Jer 44:28 Yet a small number that escape the sword shall return out of the land of Judah, and all the <u>remnant</u> of Judah, that are gone into the land of Egypt to sojourn there, shall **know** whose words shall stand, mine or theirs.

Joel 2:32 And it shall come to pass, that whosoever shall call on the name of the Lord shall be delivered for in mount Zion and in Jerusalem shall be deliverance as the Lord hath said, and in the <u>remnant</u> whom the lord shall **call.**

Amos 5:15 Hate the evil, and love the good, and establish judgment in the gate: it may be that the lord God of hosts will be **gracious** unto the <u>remnant</u> of Joseph.

Mic.2:12 I will surely assemble O Jacob, all of thee; I will surely **gather** the <u>remnant</u> of Israel; I will put them together as the sheep of Bozrah, as the flock in the midst of their fold: they shall make great noise by reason of the multitude of men.

:13 The breaker is come up before them: they have broken up and have passed through the gate, and are gone out by it: and their king shall **pass before** them, and the Lord on the **head** of them.

Mic.4:7 And I will make her that halted a remnant and her that was cast far off a strong nation: and the Lord shall **reign** over them in mount Zion from henceforth even forever.

Zeph 3:13 The remnant of Israel shall not do iniquity, nor speak lies; neither shall a deceitful tongue be found in their mouth: for they shall **feed** and **lie down**, and **none shall make them afraid**

Hag.1:12 Then Zerubbabel the son of Sheltiel, and Joshua the son of Josedech, the high priest, with all the remnant of the people, **obeyed** the voice of the Lord their God, and the word of Haggai the prophet as the lord their God had sent him, and the people did **fear** before the Lord.

:14 And the Lord stirred up the spirit of Zerubbabel the son of Sheltiel governor of Judah, and the spirit of Joshua the son of Josedech, the high priest, and the spirit of all the remnant of the people; and they came and did **work** in the house of the Lord of host, their God.

Zech 8:3 And the streets of the city shall be full of boys and girls playing in the streets thereof.

:6 Thus saith the lord of hosts; If it be marvelous in the eyes of the <u>remnant</u> of this people in these days, should it also be marvelous in mine eyes saith the Lord of hosts.

:7 Thus saith the lord behold I will **save** my people from the east country and the west country.

Rom.11:5 Even so then at this present time also there is a <u>remnant</u> according to the election of grace.

HOUR OF HARVEST

The "Ninth Hour" is an *Hour of Harvest*, where God is calling on every Bible-believing Christian to rise up to the call to preach and witness.

Mt.26:40 And he cometh unto the disciples, and findeth them asleep, and saith unto Peter, what, could ye not watch with me **one hour**?
　:41 **Watch** and **pray** that ye enter not into temptation………

Ezek 3:17 Son of man, I have made thee a **watchman** unto this house of Israel: therefore hear the word at my mouth, and give them **warning** from me.

EVIDENCES OF THE HOUR OF HARVEST

Season of the Harvest

Lk 12:56 Ye hypocrites, ye can discern the face of the sky and of the earth; but how is it that ye do not discern this time?

Jer 8:7 Yea the stork in heaven knoweth her appointed times; and the turtle and the crane and the swallow observe the time of their coming; but my people know not the judgment of the Lord

Size of the Harvest

Mth 9:38 Pray ye therefore the Lord of the harvest, that he will send forth labourers into his harvest.

Jer. 8:20 The harvest is past, the summer is ended and we are not saved

Joel 1:11 The harvest of the field is perished

Plots against Harvesters

Mk.13:9 But take heed to yourself: for they shall deliver you up to councils; and in the synagogue ye shall be beaten, and ye shall be brought before rulers and kings for my sake, for a testimony against them.
    :10 And the gospel must first be **published** among **all nations.**

Homosexual Activists, Abortionist, Secular News Media, many Politicians, Natural Healing Activists, Witchcraft Workers and Diviners, are the main agents against Harvesters in this hour.

Prophecies of the Harvest

Amos 3:7 Surely the lord God will do nothing, but He **revealeth** his secret unto his servants the prophets.
:8 The lion hath roared who will not fear? the Lord God has spoken, **who can but prophesy**?

Fulfillments of the Prophecies of the Harvest

Earthquakes, Wars , Rumors of Wars etc (Mth. 24)

GEOMETRIC MEDIA

I can hear the Lord leading the church to take a major leap ahead of the secular media to reach the world with the handful of people in it (6.7 billion).

It is so disappointing to see the major International television networks having live news and live response to the news while the church does commentary weeks later. In the midst of calamities and other history-making happenings, who is best to have up-to-the-minute communication to the people than a believer qualified to handle the subject? Our communication methods are relatively antiquated. Why is it that CNN had to be the first to show a hologram? Just imagine it being used to speak to people virtually in person anywhere in the world.

The secular media has manipulated the minds of the masses for many years. Today they feed the people with their tainted versions of happenings then conduct devious surveys and polls of the same people. **The church must become a tabernacle**

without walls where, in addition to an interactive local church service, the people actually interact with an international service even once monthly or on demand.

From Bible times, God's Word was spread by itinerant prophets and other ministers. They traveled on foot, by ass, horse, boat, ship and even chariots, to the intended places. Mail was also an integral part of sending the message. In more modern times came the use of motorized vehicles such as cars, trains, buses, and airplanes. This can be categorized by what I call '**Horizontal Media**'.

In the last hundred years, the gospel began to be spread additionally by telegraphic signals, cable systems, radio, television etc. The signal is sent up from the ground to aerial systems which is then transmitted in a diagonal manner to the corners of the earth. This can be categorized as '**Diagonal Media**'.

Today, communications have catapulted to the use of satellite and internet systems. It is now possible to conduct a church without walls from New York City to the remote jungles of the earth and vice versa. Anyone can stay in their basement and spread the gospel with more success than an established international televangelist. I call this **Vertical Media**.

Take note of how God clearly monitors the unfolding changes in media:

He prophesied that all flesh would prophesy in the last days. He first began to speak only by a few Patriarchs, Prophets and Priests. They carried the message horizontally as the population was small. As the population increased, God added more to his team to include Evangelists, Teachers, Missionaries etc; who used horizontal media.

Today, with several billions living on the earth, God has seen it fit to allow anyone who claims to know Him to prophesy to the world without personal movement or much expenditure. The secular mediums are already able to send a hologram of any person to or from any part of the world. Yet the church is still struggling to utilize the *previous inventions.*

It is evident that the end time media explosion was designed by God to evangelize the world but it has been utilized instead by the secular world. 'Wherein in time past ye walked according to the course of this world, according to the prince of the power of <u>the air</u>, the spirit that now worketh in the children of disobedience... Among whom also we all had our conversation in times past in the lusts of our flesh, fulfilling the desires of the flesh and of the mind; and were by nature the children of wrath, even as others. (Eph. 2:2,3)

But God says ' Put on the whole armor of God, that ye may be able to stand against the wiles of the devil...... for we wrestle not against flesh and blood, but against principalities, against powers, against the rulers of darkness of this world, against spiritual wickedness in <u>high places.</u>

Following, are a few scriptures demanding prior-itized use of the full geometric media to complete the mandate of world revival.

Mention:

Jer.4:5 Declare ye in Judah, and publish in Jerusalem; and say, Blow ye the trumpet in the land: cry, gather together, and say, Assemble yourselves, and let us go into the defenced cities.

:16 Make ye mention to the nations; behold, publish against Jerusalem, [that] watchers come from a far country, and give out their voice against the cities of Judah.

Declare

Jer.50:2 Declare ye among the nations, and publish, and set up a standard; publish, [and] conceal not: say, Babylon is taken, Bel is confounded, Merodach is broken in pieces; her idols are confounded, her images are broken in pieces.

:3 For out of the north there cometh up a nation against her, which shall make her land desolate, and none shall dwell therein: they shall remove, they shall depart, both man and beast.

Teach

Mth.28:19 Go ye therefore; teach all nations

Preach

Mrk.16:15 Go into all the world and preach the gospel to every creature.

Tit.1:3 But hath in due times manifested his word through preaching...

Col.1:23 If ye continue in the faith grounded and settled, and be not moved away from the hope of the gospel, which ye have heard, and which was preached to every creature which is under heaven; whereof I Paul am made a minister;

Publish

Mrk.13:9 But take heed to yourselves: for they shall deliver you up to councils; and in the synagogues ye shall be beaten: and ye shall be brought before rulers and kings for my sake, for a testimony against them.

:10 And the gospel must first be published among all nations.

Acts 13:47 For so hath the Lord commanded us, (saying), I have set thee to be a light of the Gentiles, that thou shouldest be for salvation unto the ends of the earth.

:48 And when the Gentiles heard this, they were glad, and glorified the word of the Lord: and as many as were ordained to eternal life believed

:49 And the word of the Lord was published throughout all the region.

Ps.68:11 The Lord gave the word: great was the company of those that published it.

Jer.31:7 For thus saith the Lord; Sing with gladness for Jacob, and shout among the chief of the nations: publish ye, praise ye, and say, O LORD, save thy people, the remnant of Israel.

:10 Hear the word of the LORD, O ye nations, and declare (it) in the isles afar off, and say, He that scattered Israel will gather him, and keep him, as a shepherd (doth) his flock.

Fill

Num.14:20 And the Lord said, I have pardoned according to thy word.

:21 But as truly as I live, all the earth shall be filled with the glory of the Lord.

Hab.2:14 For the earth shall be filled with the knowledge of the glory of the LORD, as the waters cover the sea.

Ps.72:19 And blessed be His glorious name for ever: and let the whole earth be filled with His glory; Amen, and Amen.

Dominate

Zech 14:9 And the Lord shall be King over all the earth: in that day shall there be one Lord, and his name one.

HOW TO BE ENLIGHTENED

HOW TO BE ENLIGHTENED

Desire

Mth 13:13 Therefore speak I to them in <u>parables</u>: because they seeing, see not and hearing they hear not, neither do they understand
:15 For this people's heart is waxed gross and their ears are dull of hearing and their <u>eyes they have closed</u>…

Fear Him

Ps.25:14 The secret of the LORD is with them that fear him; and he will shew them his covenant.

Be Filled

Jhn 16:13 …….He will shew thee things to come

Be Consumed

Dan.10:3 I ate no pleasant bread, neither came flesh nor wine in my mouth, neither did I anoint myself at all, till three whole weeks were fulfilled.

:8 Therefore I was left alone, and saw this great vision, and there remained no strength in me: for my comeliness was turned in me into corruption, and I retained no strength.

Consecrate

Ezra 9:8 And now for a little space grace hath been shewed from the LORD our God, to leave us a remnant to escape, and to give us a nail in his holy place, that our God may lighten our eyes, and give us a little reviving in our bondage.

Accompany

1Sam.10:10 And when they came thither to the hill, behold, a company of prophets met him; and the Spirit of God came upon him, and he prophesied among them.

1Sam19:20 And Saul sent messengers to take David: and when they saw the company of the prophets prophesying, and Samuel standing [as] appointed over them, the Spirit of God was upon the messengers of Saul, and they also prophesied.

Go Fishing

Ez.13:5 Ye have not <u>gone into the gaps</u>, neither made up the hedge for the house of Israel to stand in the battle in the day of the Lord.

:6 They have seen vanity and lying divination, saying The Lord saith and the Lord hath not sent them: and they have made others to hope that they would confirm the word.

Ps.107: 23-24 They that go down to the sea in ships, that do business in great waters; these see the works of the LORD, and his wonders in the deep.

Ps.77:19 Thy way is in the sea, and thy path in the great waters, and thy footsteps are not known.

Listen to the enlightened

Jer.9:12 Who is the <u>wise man</u> that may <u>understand this</u> and who is he to whom the mouth of the Lord hath spoken that he may declare it for what, the land perisheth and is burnt up

1Chr.12:32 And of the children of Issachar, which were men that had understanding of the times, to know what Israel ought to do; the heads of them [were] two hundred; and all their brethren were at their commandment.

Est.4:14 For if thou altogether holdest thy peace at this time, then shall there enlargement and deliverance arise to the Jews from another place; but thou and thy father's house shall be destroyed: and who knoweth whether thou art come to the kingdom for such a time as this?

Ps. 36:9 For with thee is the fountain of life. In thy <u>light</u>, we see <u>light</u>

Miscellaneous

Dan.2:18 That they would desire mercies of the God of heaven concerning this <u>secret</u>; that Daniel and his fellows should not perish with the rest of the wise men of Babylon.

:21 And he changeth the times and the seasons: he removeth kings, and setteth up kings: he giveth wisdom unto the wise, and knowledge to them that know understanding:

:22 He revealeth the deep and secret things: he knoweth what [is] in the darkness, and the light dwelleth with him.

:23 I thank thee, and praise thee, O thou God of my fathers, who hast given me <u>wisdom</u> and might, and hast made known unto me now what we desired of thee: for thou hast now made known unto us the king's matter.

Amos.3:7 Surely the Lord will do nothing, but he revealeth his secret unto his servants the prophets.

Daniel 2:22 He revealeth the deep and secret things: He knoweth what is in the darkness, and <u>the light</u> dwelleth with Him.

Ps.25:14 The secret of the Lord is with them that <u>fear him</u> and he <u>show</u> them his covenant.

Rev.3:22 He that hath an ear to hear, let him hear what the Spirit saith unto the churches.

Mth 13:13 Therefore speak I to them in parables: because they seeing, see not and hearing they hear not, neither do they understand
:15 For this people's heart is waxed gross and their ears are dull of hearing and their <u>eyes they have closed.</u>
;17 For verily I say unto you, that many prophets and righteous men have desired to see those things which ye see and have not seen them; and to hear those things which ye hear, and have not heard them.

Is.6:10 Make the heart of this people fat, and make their ears heavy, and shut their eyes; lest they see with their eyes, and hear with their ears, and understand with their heart, and convert, and be healed.

Jhn 16:13 … He will shew you things to come.

Joel 2:28 ....sons and daughters shall <u>prophesy</u>

Jer.8:7 Yea, the stork in the heaven knoweth her appointed times… but my people know not…

Is.30:10 ... Prophesy not unto us right things, speak unto us smooth things, prophesy deceits.

Ez.12:23 ....the days are at hand and the effect of every vision.

1Cor.14:24 But if all prophesy and there come in one that believeth not, or one unlearned, he is convinced of all, he is judged of all.
    :25 And thus are the secrets of his heart made manifest and so falling down on his face, he will worship God and report that God is in you of a truth.

Jhn.13:19 now I tell you before it comes that when it is come to pass, ye may believe.

2kg.4:16 And he said, about this season according to the time of life, thou shalt embrace a son: and she said, nay my Lord thou man of God, <u>do not lie</u> to thy handmaid.
    :17 And the woman conceived; and bare a son at the season that Elisha had said unto her according to the time of life.

Job 12:25 They grope in the dark without <u>light</u>...

1Kg.22:8 And the king of Israel said unto Jehoshaphat, there is yet one man......but I hate him for he doth not prophesy good concerning me but evil.

Dan.9:22 And he(Gabriel) informed me, and talked with me, and said, O Daniel, I am now come to give thee <u>skill and understanding</u>

:23 And at the beginning of thy supplications the commandment came forth, and I am come to <u>shew thee</u>; for thou art greatly beloved: therefore <u>understand</u> the matter and <u>consider the vision</u>.

NINTH HOUR FIRE

Repair the Altar

By having a:
- Special Place for prayer
- 1- 3 Hours of Daily Prayer (This may involve meditation on God and His word and writing revelations received)

1Kg.18:30 And Elijah said unto all the people, come near unto me And all the people came near unto him, and he repaired the altar of the Lord that was broken down

Tarry at the Altar

By spending quality time in hours, days, months if necessary.

Acts 1:4 And, being assembled together with [them], commanded them that they should not depart from

Jerusalem, but <u>wait for the promise</u> of the Father, which, [saith he], ye have heard of me.

Intensify the Heat

-   <u>Two days of regular fasting weekly</u>: One day each, before Sunday services and mid-week services
-   <u>Generally increase fasting from</u> 1 day to 3 days, 7 days, 21 days, 30 days, 40 days. Each year you climb to the next level and so on.

Eat Fire

-   <u>Memorize:</u> fiery scriptures
-   <u>Read</u>: the Bible through several times; at least every 3 years
-   <u>Listen</u> to fiery sermons.

Isa.6:6 Then one of the seraphim flew to me, having in his hand a live coal [which] he had taken with the tongs from the altar.

:7 And he touched my mouth [with it], and said: "Behold, this has touched your lips; Your iniquity is taken away, And your sin purged."

<u>Ez</u>.3:1 Moreover he said unto me, Son of man, eat that thou findest; eat this roll, and go speak unto the house of Israel

Jer.20:9 Then I said, I will not make mention of him, nor speak any more in his name. But [his word] was

in mine heart as a burning fire shut up in my bones, and I was weary with forbearing, and I could not [stay]..

Absorb the Heat

- <u>Meditate</u> on the fiery word

For example if you are chosen to minister the Word at your church or to pray for the sick, you can't be coming from shopping just before preaching time; just finish cooking or just coming off the long phone call before you do this task. You should prepare for this moment and ignore other good things for maximum effect.

Joshua 1:8 This book of the law shall not depart out of thy mouth; but thou shalt meditate therein day and night...

Burn in the Gaps

- Preaching / Witnessing in the streets, homes etc. at least once weekly

Ez.13:5 Ye have not gone up into the gaps...

Jer.20:9 But his word was in mine heart as a burning fire shut up in my bones...

Burn Heresy

Jer. 5:12 They have belied the Lord...

Time Programmed

1Sam 21:8 The kings business require haste

Focus on Mandate
The ultimate call for World Revival; nothing less, no substitute.

Ph.3:14 Press towards the mark for the prize of the high calling of God in Christ Jesus.
-   Evaluate whether you are prepared to be a gifted: <u>idler, loser, survivor, runner up</u> or <u>finalist</u>
-   The call should take precedence over personal <u>ambition</u>
-   <u>Step aside</u>/ make sacrifices for the collective good of the Mandate (for e.g. In the Pensacola revival, the Pastor stepped aside and allowed the Evangelist to lead the church for a season)
-   Be aware of <u>Distraction</u>: by relatives and friends (be 'relative proof')
-   Cancel previous <u>appointments</u> for momentous request & expectations
-   <u>Spouse:</u> Clarify spouse's <u>Participation.</u> Is he/she allowed to cross God's dealing with you. Do you wilt to their <u>demand, desires</u> and sometimes <u>blackmail</u> at the expense of the

call? (Ezekiel's wife did not interfere with his call but God allowed her to die because he was distracted by her Ez.24:16-18)

Serve a Flaming Fire

Be an Armor bearer to God's ministers-for e.g. your Pastor, Bishop (Heb.1:7, Ex..24:13, Josh.1:1

Integrity

- Fulfill /honor your Obligations
- Be faithful in your Tithing & Offering
- Financial Blamelessness
- Do not be afraid to go to the altar
- Do not be afraid to get baptized again if you feel an urge

Scandal Proof

- Opposite Sex
- Handling of Money

INVISIBLE
WARFARE

Many years ago, patients died because doctors did not particularly wash their hands before doing surgery or even maternity delivery. When bacteria were discovered among the many other microscopic organisms, the death toll was virtually stopped by basic hygiene such as washing the hands.

The past three(3) years (2005 –2007) have seen more Christian ministers fall disgracefully or damaged dramatically than any other period in history. This includes thousands of Christian leaders across the world leading hundreds of millions of people, International heads of Church denominations, Mega – churches, Christian television networks, established prophets. It is certainly numbered in the thousands worldwide.

Each time these things happen, other ministers try to diagnose the reasons, publish them, then move on. Then more falling occurs, then more diagnoses, then more falling; it would seem like a continuous cycle. Anyone can produce a convincing diagnosis after the fact. However, the best persons to seek answers from are those who prophesied **BEFORE** that these things would happen (see the prophecy page on harvestarmy.org).

Just like bacteria and virus multiply microscopically if one's hands are not washed, one's spiritual life deteriorates when he/she disregards God's guidelines for living pure and holy before Him. The Body of Christ has been doing many things which *seem* harmless but they have done gradual microscopic damage and death to our spiritual lives. We have disregarded the many safety mechanisms given by God, labeling them as *legalism, tradition, religion* and even *curses.*

Certain environments are more conducive to bacterial growth than others. Similarly, in the spiritual world, wicked sins are created and made virtually unmovable by certain seemingly harmless but un-biblical environments or mediums. The following is not exhaustive but some of the mediums that may have been missed:

OLD TESTAMENT RITUALS

2Cor.3:14 But their minds were **blinded**: for until **this day** remaineth the same vail untaken away in the reading of the **Old Testament** ; which vail is **done away** in Christ.

:15 But even until **this day** when Moses is read the vail is **upon their heart**

<u>Gal. 4:9</u> …..how turn ye again to the **beggarly** elements whereunto ye desire again to be in bondage

<u>:10</u> Ye observe **days** and **months**, and **times** and **years**.

Gal.2:14 But when I saw that they walked not uprightly according to the truth of the gospel, I said unto Peter before them all *(public rebuke of an elder because of the serious wrong)*. If thou being a Jew, livest after the manner of the Gentiles and not as do the Jews, why compellest thou the Gentiles to live as the Jews.

:18 For if I build again the things which I destroyed, I make myself a **<u>trangressor</u>**

:21 …..if righteousness come by the law, then Christ is dead in vain

- Observing Jewish feasts
- Praying with Shawl
- Praying at the Wailing Wall
- Blowing of Shofars etc.
- Bowing to a Mercy Seat asking for mercy
- Jewish-type worship for Christians
- Kosher Diet for spirituality
- Display of Menorah
- Burning of incense, candles etc.
- Catholic Confessions
- Sabbathism: Mk.2:27,28; Col.2:16

EASTERN ENCHANTMENT

Is.2:6 Therefore thou hast forsaken thy people the house of Jacob, because they be replenished from the East, and are soothsayers like the Philistines.

Rom 14:2 For one believeth that he may eat all things: another, who is weak, eateth herbs.

:17 For the kingdom of God is not meat and drink; but righteousness, and peace, and joy in the Holy Ghost.

1Tim 4:3 Forbidding to marry and commanding to **abstain from meats** which God hath created to be received with thanksgiving of them which believe and know the truth

- Vegetarianism
- Natural Healing
- Un-biblical Meditation (for e.g. yoga)
- Aspects of Karate

GENDER CROSSROAD

Deut.22:5 The woman shall not **wear** what pertaineth unto **a man**. neither shall a man put on a **womans garment:** for all that do so are **abomination** unto the Lord.

Ex.29:42 And thou shalt make them linen **breeches** to cover their nakedness from the loins even unto the thighs they shall reach.

:43 And they shall be upon **Aaron**, and upon his **sons**.......

Lev. 6:10 And the priest shall put on his linen garment, and his linen **breeches** shall he put upon his flesh, and take up the ashes which the fire hath consumed with the burnt offering on the altar, and he shall put them beside the altar.

Lev.16:4 He shall put on the holy linen coat, and he shall have the linen **breeche**s upon his flesh, and shall be girded with a linen girdle, and with the linen mitre shall he be attired: these [are] holy garments; therefore shall he wash his flesh in water, and so put them on.

In the Hebrew lexicon, **breeches** mean **trousers** that extend to the knee, below the knee, or to the ankles." This would include pants, shorts, or culottes.

- Strange Apparel (Cross Dressing): Jude 1:7; Zeph.1:8
- Absence of distinguishing roles.
  - <u>Men</u> - *Provision* 1Tim.5:8
  - <u>Women</u> - *Care* Prv.31:13-21
- Long hair males 1.Cor.11:14
- Intentional short hair women 1Cor.11:15

WORLDLINESS

<u>Jam.4:3</u> Ye ask, and receive not, because ye ask amiss, that ye may consume it upon your **lust**.

:4 ye adulterers and adulteresses, know ye not that the friendship of the world is enmity with God? whosoever therefore will be a **friend** of the **world** is the **enemy** of God

- Cinemas
- Secular Music
- "Heathen Gospel Singers" in churches
- Dating too long before marriage
- Unnecessary Jewelry
- Ostentation
- Heathens as best friend
- Organized dancing ministry (different from personally dancing in the Spirit like David)

DIVINATION MEDIUMS

➤ Acts 16:16 Woman possessed with spirit of divination

➤ Acts 8 Simon of Samaria: Could not receive the Holy Spirit

- Circle Prayer
- Water drinking for healing in church services
- Worshipping, praying in the dark deliberately.
- Horoscope
- Chain letters
- Psychic Association (for e.g. calling psychic hotline, palm reading

DOCTRINES OF DEVILS

Acts 4:12 Neither is there salvation in any other for there is **none other name** under heaven given among men whereby ye must be saved

- Pluralism, Universalism
- Unconditional Security(Once saved Always saved)
- Animism (Ancestor worship, cultural Gospel)
- Suicidal Hope (Christians who commit suicide go to heaven)
- Prosperity Righteousness
- Denigrating the old path
- Dual Covenant (Jews get to heaven despite rejecting Jesus)
- Cultural Gospel
- One-sided preaching (deliberate omission of certain sins in sermons)

Here is a conditional prophecy that will mostly be disregarded. 'Believers who embrace any of the above environments will bear the fruit of sin, failure and disaster'.

In our rebellion against God we have tainted the name of the holiness churches which most times are already conscious of the need to beware of these agents of (the) "Invisible Warfare". Some worldly-wise preachers have gone as far as to label clear New Testament instructions as *legalism, tradition, religion* or even a *curse*. It is not surprising to observe that such preachers and or their sheep are the ones who mainly fall later on.

The fruit is the eventual proof of what seed was planted. What are you doing in a church with:

- More than 20% Divorce,
- Multiple marriage pulpits,
- Uni-sexism,
- Light preaching (sin omission) ,
- Preponderance of Adultery, fornication, homosexuality etc
- Preponderance of depression, mental illness, drug addiction, suicide?

What are you doing in a church with the above fruits? Why are you looking for healthy oranges in a germy swamp? Get out before bad fruits are birthed in you. If you are already caught, be loosed in Jesus' name! Storm into a Holiness Church and renounce your past life.

God's equity demands judgment upon the church and the world. Many more delusional bubbles will burst in the church and the world as they embrace the mediums of Invisible Warfare against us. Make your calling and election sure!

Acts 17:30 And the times of this ignorance God **winked** at; but now commandeth all men everywhere to repent.

:31 Because he hath appointed a day, in the which he will judge the world in righteousness by that man whom he hath ordained; whereof He hath given **assurance** unto all men, in that He hath raised him from the dead.

Jer 23:20 The anger of the Lord shall not return till he have executed. In the **latter days** thou shalt **consider it perfectly**

MORE SCRIPTURES

Ps.74:7 They have **cast fire** into thy sanctuary, they have **defiled** by casting down the dwelling place of thy name to the ground.

Ezek.20:38 And I will **purge** out from among you the **rebels** and them that transgress against me......

Jer.3:3 Therefore the **showers have been withholden**, and there hath been **no latter rain**; and thou hadst a whore's forehead, thou refusedst to be ashamed.

Jhn 12:48 He that rejecteth me, and receiveth not my words, hath one that judgeth him: **the word** that I have spoken, the same shall **judge** him in the last day

Rev.20:12 And I saw the dead, small and great stand before God: and the books were opened: and another book was opened, which is the **book of life**: and the dead were judged out of those things which were **written in the books**, according to their **works**

Rom. 14:10 ...for **we shall all stand before** the judgment seat of Christ.

:12 So then every one of us shall give account of himself to God

Is.4:4 When the Lord shall have washed away the filth of the daughters of Zion, and shall have purged the blood of Jerusalem from the midst thereof by the **spirit of judgment**, and by the **spirit of burning**

1Cor.2:4,5 My speech and my preaching was not with **enticing words** of man's wisdom but with **demonstration** of the spirit and of **power.**
:5 That your faith should not stand in the **wisdom of men** but in the **power of God**.

Josh 7:12 .... neither will I be with you any more, except ye destroy the **accursed** from among you.

2Th.2 Church deceived just before Christ return.

Ez.9:4 Set a mark upon the foreheads of the men that sigh and that cry for all **abominations**
:6 Slay.......but come not near anyman upon whom is the mark

Lev.18:3 After the doings of the land of Egypt, wherein ye dwelt, shall ye not do and after the doings of the land of Canaan whither I bring you, shall ye not do, neither shall ye walk in their ordinances
:25 And the land is **defiled**...

Prv.28:9 He that turneth his ear away from hearing the law even his **prayer** shall be an **abomination**

Eccl.1:18 In much wisdom is much grief. he that increaseth knowledge increaseth sorrow

Ezek. 13:18 ….. woe to the women that sew pillows to all armholes, and make kerchiefs upon the head of every stature to hunt souls!
:19 ….to slay the souls that should not die and save the souls that should not live…

Ps. 50:16 But unto the wicked God saith, what hast thou to do to **declare my statutes**, or that thou shouldest take my covenant in thy mouth.

Ex.19:5,6 ….ye shall be unto me a **peculiar people**: for all the earth is mine.
:6 And ye shall be unto me a kingdom of **priest**.

Eccl 5:9 The **profit** of the earth is for **all**

1Sam.8:7 They have not rejected thee, but they have **rejected me**, that I should not reign over them.

Prv.15:10 Correction is grievious to him that **forsaketh the way** and he that hate reproof shall **die**

1Tim.6:4 He is **proud knowing nothing** but doting about questions and **strifes of words.**

Jer.15:19 …Thus saith the Lord. If thou return then will I bring thee again…… if thou take forth the precious from the vile thou shalt be as **my mouth**. Let them return but return not unto them

Titus 3:10 A man that is a **heretic** after the first and second admonition, **reject.**

:11 Knowing that he that is such is **subverted** and **sinneth** being **condemned** of himself.

NINTH HOUR
READINESS

During the ninth hour it is wise to be in 'Safe Mode', It may even be necessary to temporarily 'Retreat' in some areas of your life. The term 'Hunker Down' might be fitting in some areas. It is important to simultaneously 'Focus' on what matters when everything else fails)

INDIVIDUALLY

Communication

- Get email account if you have none
- Check Prophecy page (<u>harvestarmy.org</u>)
- Update contact information (telephone # & address) with your church
- Check email daily
- Don't miss church

Calculate Degree of Urgency: (State of)

- Awareness
- Alert
- Alarm

First Necessities

- Food (non-perishables, baby foods)
- Water
- Housing
- Shelter (Where to go if evacuation becomes necessary)
- Energy (for movement, light, cooking)
- Cash
- Battery radio
- Flashlight

Secure your Job

- Work Harder
- Arrive on time
- Reduce complaints

Housing

- Stay put where you are unless going to share housing with a relative or friend
- Don't rush to purchase until the uncertainties subside

Money

- Retain more cash by utilizing credit
- Delay or drop bills that are possible
- Sell extra vehicle or return it
- Travel less
- Simpler Ceremonies (weddings, birthdays etc.)

CORPORATELY

Amalgamate

- Churches merge for greater World Revival impact
- United Groceries Pantry: Mainly non-perishables)
- Joint ventures, arrangements between brethren (for e.g. businesses, housing, combining resources)

Reduced Employment

- Employers may have to lay off some staff
- Employers may employ workers for less hours

ECONOMIC SOLUTIONS

Deut.8:18 But thou shalt remember the LORD thy God: for it is he that **giveth thee power to get wealth**, that he may establish his covenant which he sware unto thy fathers, as (it is) this day

Is.45:17 Thus saith the LORD, thy Redeemer, the Holy One of Israel; I am the LORD thy God which **teacheth thee to profit**, which leadeth thee by the way [that] thou shouldest go.

3Jhn.1:2 Beloved, I wish above all things that thou mayest **prosper** and be in health, even as **thy soul prospereth**.

Eccl.10:19 A feast is made for laughter, and wine maketh merry: but **money answereth all things.**

....

BELIEVE GOD'S PROPHETS

Ezra 6:14 And the elders of the Jews builded, and they **prospered through the prophesying** of **Haggai** the prophet and **Zechariah** the son of Iddo. And they builded, and finished it, according to the commandment of the God of Israel, and according to the commandment of Cyrus, and Darius, and Artaxerxes king of Persia.

2Chr.20:20 And they rose early in the morning, and went forth into the wilderness of Tekoa: and as they went forth, Jehoshaphat stood and said, Hear me, O Judah, and ye inhabitants of Jerusalem; Believe in the LORD your God, so shall ye be established; **believe his prophets**, so shall ye **prosper**

GIVE BOUNTIFULLY TO GOD

Prv.21:25,26 .....the righteous giveth and spareth not

Mal.3:10 **Bring ye all the tithes** into the **storehouse**, that there may be **meat in mine house**, and **prove me** now herewith, saith the LORD of hosts, if I will not **open you the windows** of heaven, and pour you out a **blessing**, that there shall not be room enough to receive it.

11: And I will **rebuke the devourer** for your sakes, and he shall **not destroy** the fruits of your ground; neither shall your vine cast her fruit **before the time** in the field, saith the LORD of hosts.

Lk.6:38 **Give,** and it shall be **given** unto you; **good** measure, **pressed** down, and **shaken** together, and **running** over, shall men give into your bosom. For with the same measure that ye mete withal it shall be measured to you again.

2Cor.9:6_But this I say, He which soweth sparingly shall reap also sparingly; and he which **soweth bountifully** shall reap also **bountifully**.

BE ALERT

Jer 45: 5 And seekest thou great things for thyself? seek (them) not: for, behold, I will bring evil upon all flesh, saith the LORD: but thy **life** will I give unto thee for a **prey** in all places whither thou goest.

* Store non-perishable foods, basic energy, light, battery radio, cash, petrol in vehicle, etc.

SAVE WISELY

Gen.41:36 And that food shall be for **store** to the land against the seven years of **famine**, which shall be in the land of Egypt; that the land perish not through the **famine**.

Prv.13:22 A good man leaveth an **inheritance** to his children's children: and the **wealth** of the sinner is laid up for the just.

TRADE WISELY

Prv.31:16 She considereth a field, and buyeth it: with the fruit of her hands she planteth a vineyard.

Mth.15:16 Then he that had received the **five talents** went and **traded** with the same, and made (them) other **five talents**.

Luk.14;28 For which of you, intending to build a tower, sitteth not down first, and counteth the **cost**, whether he have (sufficient) to finish (it)?

- Instead of hoarding what you will never use, sell it or donate it to the church
- Internet Business
- Barter
- Look for bargains
- United garage sale

BE CONTENT

.
Heb.13:5 Let your conversation be without covetousness; and **be content** with such things as ye have: for he hath said, I will never leave thee, nor forsake thee.
- Main necessities are: sufficient shelter, food and clothing
- Inexpensive items: vehicle, home, things
- Economical activities: simpler weddings, birthday parties etc.
- Less activities: for e.g; Reduce travel- vacations

- Less vehicles
- Energy reduction in housing, vehicle
- Recycle

DO PARTNERSHIP

Acts 4:32 And the multitude of them that believed were of **one heart** and of **one soul**: neither said any of them that ought of the things which he possessed was his own; but they had **all things common**.
- Used items, clothes, books, cars (are sometimes better than new)
- Come together and purchase some things such as cars
- Employ your brethren
- 2 Families live in one house
- Give reduced charge or free time to your brethren (baby sitting, business etc)
- Supermarket, hairdressing and barbershop businesses etc.
- Barter
- No interest loans
- Partnership saving
- Renting from each other

BE SOBER

1Pet.5:8 Be **sober**, be vigilant; because your adversary the devil, as a roaring lion, walketh about, **seeking whom he may devour**:

MISCELLANEOUS

More Ninth Hour Scriptures

1Kg 18:36 And it came to pass at the time of the offering of the <u>evening sacrifice</u>, that Elijah the prophet came near, and said, LORD God of Abraham, Isaac, and of Israel, let it be known this day that thou [art] God in Israel, and [that] I [am] thy servant, and [that] I have done all these things at thy word.

:38 Then the fire of the LORD fell, and consumed the burnt sacrifice, and the wood, and the stones, and the dust, and licked up the water that [was] in the trench.

Dan.9:21 Yea, whiles I was speaking in prayer, even the man Gabriel, whom I had seen in the vision at the beginning, being caused to fly swiftly, touched me about the time of the <u>evening oblation</u>.

Ezra.9:5 And at the <u>evening sacrifice</u> I arose up from my heaviness; and having rent my garment and my mantle, I fell upon my knees, and spread out my hands unto the LORD my God.

:6 And said, O my God, I am ashamed and blush to lift up my face to thee, my God: for our iniquities are increased over our head, and our trespass is grown up unto the heavens.

Acts 10:30 And Cornelius said, Four days ago I was fasting until this hour; and at the <u>ninth hour</u> I prayed in my house, and, behold, a man stood before me in bright clothing.

:31 And said, Cornelius, thy prayer is heard, and thine alms are had in remembrance in the sight of God.

(Mth 27:45-51, Josh 7:6 – 10)

<u>NINE LETTER PLACES TODAY</u>

It would be wise to pay attention to the countries having nine letters. It is interesting that there are presently 18 sovereign countries with 9 letters (1 + 8 = 9)

Sovereign Countries

> Argentina
> Australia
> Cape Verde
> Costa Rica
> East Timor

Guatemala
Indonesia
Nicaragua
Lithuania
Macedonia
Mauritius   `
Palestine
San Marino
Singapore
Swaziland
The Gambia (smallest country in Africa)
Venezuela

Non-Sovereign Countries

Isle of Man
Gibraltar
Greenland

Harvest Army Church Int'l

It is quite notable how 'Harvest Army World Revival Movement', the ministry I lead, is connected to the number "nine".

Ezekiel 37:10 is the golden Text of the vision from the time of the revelation of the vision.
'So I prophesied as He commanded me, and the breath came into them, and they lived, and stood upon there feet an exceeding great army.
  # *'**Exceeding Great Army***' (18 letters: 1 + 8 = **9**).

Every Saturday the whole church is sent to preach on the streets of New York City including the square of the world 'Times Square'. This is also done world-wide in branches and affiliates. The activity on Saturday is called 'Saturday Storm'. It is also called 'Preach Out' to include other days

   # *'Preach Out'* (9 letters).

The name of our International headquarters Sanctuary is called 'World Revival Center'.

   # *'World Revival Center'* (18 letters: 1 + 8 = **9**)

Many great church leaders got caught in year 2,000 AD with Y2K but prophecy came forth in Harvest Army Church Int'l of **2001** being the year to watch. On September 6, **2001** a group of us left New York City to open a new Headquarters in Texas. Five days later, (September 11), the bombing of the historical World Trade Center took place.

   # 9 . 6 . 2001 9 + 6 + 2 + 1 = 18; 1 + 8 = **9**),

. . . .

PROPHECY PAGE
WWW.HARVESTARMY.ORG
April 11, 2009

Even a 'Prophetic Footprint' (general prophecy) is greater than great analytic sermons. Thousands in New York City and New Orleans would have been saved by even a prophetic footprint.
(see bottom of page)
Fulfillments are posted for prophecies already posted on this page only. They are copied to the top of the page as soon as there is evidence of fulfillment. Prophecies are never backdated, never altered, never removed after being posted.

With Christian love, we sorrow for those who suffer in fulfillments regardless of the circumstances involved.

....

Though there are no alterations on the actual prophecies on the web site, there are a few omissions in this book. Also a few fulfillments have been altered in terms of actual names of persons.

PRESIDENTIAL ADVICE 9/9/2003

REVELATION:

- August 2003 The Islamic Terrorist are **not the main threat**. They are like **worms** on a hook. As soon as they are devoured, the **fish** which devours them will be hooked. The greater task is to identify the **fisherman** who throws out the hook.

Explanation: The fish is the **USA.** The worm is the **terrorist**. The fisherman is **'The Beast'** of the book of Revelation. This beast comes in four(4) forms, a being, a spirit, a **political system**, and an image. The political system is a group of **nations**. These nations indirectly assist the terrorist to weary the USA emotionally, economically and militarily. As soon as the USA is weak enough, they will strike.

PRIESTLY ADVICE

REVELATION:
- September 9, 2002 The **'Natural Healing'** wave that you embrace is a mask to widen the door to **pluralism, idolatry and witchcraft** in the Body of Christ. If you do not stop, your ministries will be **entrapped, damaged** or **destroyed**.

Explanation: Isaiah 2:6, 1Tim.4:3, Rom.14:2-3, Isaiah 59:8-10 etc.

HEADLINES

PROPHECY: **'NINTH HOUR'**
- July 24, 2004 God has revealed the number <u>NINE (9)</u> as the <u>Prophetic Number</u> for the last of the last days. (The interpretation of this is that the count-down to the showdown' between good and evil has began. This number will be evident in many **future happenings**
FULFILLMENT :
- April 5, 09 Worst Earthquake in Italy since 1980. 15,000 buildings destroyed or damaged; Over 300 dead; Tens of thousands homeless

    9:30 PM (EST)

    6.3 on Richter's scale (6 + 3 = **9**)

    8.8 Kilometers dee9 (approx **9**)
- April 3, 2009 Gun - Massacre in New York, Binghampton. 14 Dead, 4 Wounded

    45 Caliber rifle (4 + 5 = **9**)

    9 Millimeter gun

    18 people shot including gunner. (1 + 8 = **9**)
- Feb. 4, 09 Iran launches satellite into space for first time.

    # **SATELLITE** 9 letters
- Feb. 4, 09 North Korea prepares to test missile labeled 'Taepodong 2' , Can land in the USA

    # **TAEPODONG** 9 letters
- Feb. **4,** 09 **9**0,000 Sex offenders removed from internet social sites

- Feb. 4, 09 **9** Million dollars stolen from ATM worldwide
- Feb. 4, 09 USA Stimulus Bill reaches **9**00 Billion dollars
- Jan. 15, 2009: **US AIRWAYS** Plane Crash in Hudson River, **MANHATTAN,** New York on its way from **LA GUARDIA** airport to **CHARLOTTE** on (**1. 15. 2009**)
    # **US AIRWAYS 9** letters
    # **MANHATTAN 9** letters
    # **LA GUARDIA 9** letters
    # **CHARLOTTE 9** letters
    # **1. 15. 2009 18** total (1 + 8 = **9**)
- Jan. 2009 Earthquake in **COSTA RICA** kills at least 40
    # **COSTA RICA 9** letters

PROPHECY: Feb. 16, 09 "Oh that my head were waters, and mine eyes a fountain of tears, that I might weep day and night for the slain of the daughter of my people......... For **DEATH IS COME UP INTO OUR WINDOWS,** and is entered in our palaces, to cut off the children from without, and the young men from the streets....Even the carcasses of men shall fall as dung upon the open field, and as the handful after the harvestman, and none shall gather them....."
FULFILLMENT: April 3, 2009 Gun - Massacre in **NEW YORK,** UPPER-STATE, BINGHAMPTON. **14 Dead**, 4 Wounded

PROPHECY: Sept. 18, 07 Vision of massive use of **GUNS** for terrorism
FULFILLMENT: April 3, 2009 Gun - Massacre in **NEW YORK,** UPPER-STATE, BINGHAMPTON. **14 Dead**, 4 Wounded
Nov. 26, 08 Terrorist attack in Mumbai, India - 171 dead, hundreds injured, Anti-terror chief killed

PROPHECY: Oct. 22, 2006 Crime rate will increase in New York. Young people will terrorize. **GUN WILL BE USED LIKE A TOY**
FULFILLMENT: April 3, 2009 Gun - Massacre in **NEW YORK,** UPPER-STATE, BINGHAMPTON. **14 Dead**, 4 Wounded

PROPHECY April 7, 2009 A Hispanic Riot will break out in the Americas.

PROPHECY: March 19, 09 Thus saith the Lord, **'RING THE BELL':**
THE BELL:
Biblical Prophecies:
Signs of the times:
Personal Prophecies: (# NINTH HOUR # NEW CHAPTER # 2007 - 2009 WILL BE A SEASON OF 'GOD'S JUDGMENT' # ONE DAY # I AM THAT I AM # A VISITATION OF JUDGMENT IS IMMINENT)

PROPHECY: Feb. 25, 09 Riots in South America

PROPHECY: Oct. 29, 07 Small aircraft crash in populated area
PROPHECY: Feb. 13, 09 Small aircraft crash in populated area in Buffalo, New York. 50 dead
Nov.4, 08 Small aircraft (Lear 45) with 9 passengers crashes in Mexico City at 6:45 p.m. in rush traffic. All on board dies plus 5 people from the ground

PROPHECY: January 18, 2007 A vehicle like weapon sails into the sky to cause much carnage. Siberia - Russia - A Middle Eastern Country indicated *(Prophetess J. Hall)*
FULFILLMENT: Feb, 2009 Satellites from Russia & USA collide over Siberia. The shattered materials are said to be a collision risk to other satellites and potential tragedy on the ground

PROPHECY: Feb, 11, 09 **'A visitation of judgment is imminent'** on Adultery, Treachery, Lying, , Evil, Backsliding, Supplanting, Slander, Deception, Iniquity, Wretchedness, Conspiracy, Disobedience, Arrogance, Idolatry, Hypocrisy. Death, trials, wormwood, scattering, confusion etc is imminent (vision of Jeremiah 9)

PROPHECY: Feb. 11, 09 'South America will be stretched' especially the Southern part. A woman calls for revival.
FULFILLMENT: Feb.16, 09 Venezuela remove term limits from constitution allowing President Hugo Chavez the possibility to stay in power for the rest of his life.

PROPHECY: Feb, 11, 09 'A visitation of judgment is imminent' on Adultery, Treachery, Lying, , Evil, Backsliding, Supplanting, Slander, Deception, Iniquity, Wretchedness, Conspiracy, Disobedience, Arrogance, Idolatry, Hypocrisy. Death, trials, wormwood, scattering, confusion etc is imminent (vision of Jeremiah 9)

PROPHECY: Feb. 11, 09 'South America will be stretched' especially the Southern part. A woman calls for revival.

PROPHECY:
- Jan. 2, 09 Thus saith the Lord, In '**ONE DAY**'
    # Sorcerers, Enchanters, Associates will experience judgment and loss of offspring & widowhood.
    # Spiritual Giants who have forsaken the only way of Christ Lord will be judged

PROPHECY
- Jan. 2 2009 Thus saith the Lord '**I AM THAT I AM**'
    # Enemies of the Cross will be heart hardened, offspring struck, one fire to another, unable to buffet as before, shame, blasphemers will give account in desolation; Lewdness and idolatry will incur calamity
    # Swarms of flies shall not be nigh my people. They will receive treasures of darkness and secret places, eat meat, bread and gain victory.

PROPHECY
- Jan. 2, 2009 Resolution against true Christianity

PROPHECY
- Jan. 2, 2009 Jewish war against enemies.

PROPHECY
- Jan. 2, 2009 Fire will come upon Russia

PROPHECY
- Jan. 2, 2009 The waters will be struck

PROPHECY:
- Jan. 3, 2009 Many laymen will arise preaching the gospel

PROPHECY
- Nov. 25, 2006 A vision reveals **INDIA** under attack.
FUFILLMENTL:
- Nov. 26, 08 Terrorist attack in Mumbai, India - 171 dead, hundreds injured, Anti-terror chief killed

PROPHECY:
- June 11, 08 CHAOS IN ASIA: Politicians step down; Immoral revelry. Theft/run on banks; Gate of relief about to close.
FULFILLMENT:
- Nov. 26, 08 Terrorist attack in Mumbai, India - 171 dead, hundreds injured, Anti-terror chief killed
- Nov. 26, 08 International Airport in Thailand taken over and shut down by citizens. They call for the prime Minister to step down.

- Oct. 6, 08 'Panic about how the US and European governments have not yet found a solution to the plague sweeping through the global financial system, hit Asian stocks.......'*(REUTERS)*
- Oct. 6, 08 'Markets responded to the disarray by sinking rapidly, following sell offs in Asia. Russia shut down both it's stock market after they fell more than 15 percent' *(AP)*
Sept. 08 'ASIAN HEADS OF GOVERNMENT STEP DOWN' prematurely at record pace (Thailand, Japan, Nepal, Pakistan, Israel)
- Aug. 20, 2008 Russia invades Georgia, remains despite claims of withdrawal
- Aug. 20, 2008 Pakistan President (Musharraf) steps down amid threat of impeachment

PROPHECY:
- Sept. 18, 07 Vision of massive use of **GUNS** for terrorism
FULFILLMENT:
- Nov. 26, 08 Terrorist attack in Mumbai, <u>India</u> - 171 dead, hundreds injured, Anti-terror chief killed

PROPHECY
- Dec. 2002 An **UNDERGROUND FORCE** being formed.
FULFILLMENT:
- Nov.4, 08 Announcement of 'National Civilian Security Force' to be formed. This was a total surprise to the nation.
- April 2004 Announcement of leader needed for secret police.

PROPHECY:
- Oct. 29, 07 Small aircraft crash in populated area
FULFILLMENT:
- Nov.4, 08 Small aircraft (Lear 45) with 9 passengers crashes in Mexico City at 6:45 PM. in rush traffic. All on board dies plus 5 people from the ground

PROPHECY:
- Sept. 27, 2005 New pages are being turned on the earth. A **NEW CHAPTER** is about to unfold on the earth. What is unknown will not prevent the dramatic **CHANGES**. They will be rapid and will have the drama of a new season or a sub-dispensation.
FULFILLMENT:
- Jan. 30, 2009 Michael Steele, first black man to be voted Chairman of the Republican Party in the USA
- Feb. 2, 2009 Eric Holder, the first black man confirmed as Attorney General for the USA.
- Feb. 1, 2009 Johanna Sigurdardottir became the first female Prime Minister of Iceland.
- Feb. 2, 2009 Muammar Abu Minyar al-Gaddafi of Libya was named head of the African Union for a year. (politically isolated worldwide for decades for alleged role in terrorism)
- Nov. 4, 2008: 1st black man Barack Obama elected as next USA President, with his theme 'CHANGE'
- Jan. 26, 2006 'Hamas' wins landslide election in Palestine (Terrorist group sworn to wipe Israel off the map). Fox Television calls it 'Political Earthquake'. CNN call it 'The Earthquake Richter did not predict'. Hamas leader vows to liberate all their land

- Oct. 26, 2005 Iran's President calls for Israel to be wiped off the map

PROPHECY: **'NINTH HOUR'**
- July 24, 2004 God has revealed the number <u>NINE</u> <u>(9)</u> as the <u>Prophetic Number</u> for the last of the last days. (The interpretation of this is that the countdown to the showdown' between good and evil has began. This number will be evident in many **FUTURE HAPPENINGS** *(repeat)*
FULFILLMENT:
- Nov. 26, 08 Terrorist attack in Mumbai, <u>India</u> - 171 dead, hundreds injured, Anti-terror chief killed
    # 171 killed 1 + 7 + 1 = 9
    # Main perpetrators suspected by India:
    # ZAKI-UN-REHMANLAKTUS 18 letters 1 + 8 = 9
    # HAVAS-MOHAMMED SAAED 18 letters 1 + 8 = 9
- Nov .4, 08. 6:45 p.m. Small aircraft (Lear 45) with 9 passengers crashes in Mexico City in rush traffic. All on board dies plus 5 people from the ground.
    # Lear 45. 4 + 5 = 9
- Nov. 4, 2008: 11:30 P.M., Barack Obama elected as next USA President , Speaks to the nation at midnight
    # <u>President</u> - (9 letters)
    # <u>Barack Hussein Obama:</u> 18 letters (1 + 8 = 9)
    # 2009: <u>9th Year </u>of new millennium - Inauguration
    # 'Nomination Speech' exactly <u>45 Years</u> since Martin Luther King's 'Dream Speech'. (4 + 5 = 9)

1st Press Conference(Nov.7, 08), appeared with exactly 17 leaders. (President(1) + 17 = 18) (1 + 8 = 9)

Inherits 'Recession' 9 letters

- Sept. 12, 08 *HurricaneIke bring much destruction to Texas & Louisiana*

   # *HURRICANE - 9 letters*

   # *Main Part of Texas: GALVESTON - 9 letters*

   # *Last major hurricane 108 years ago. 1 + 0 + 8 = 9*

   # *Louisiana also hit greatly: LOUISIANA: 9 letters*

- July 2008 *Earthquake in Los Angeles:*

   # *5.4 magnitude (5+4=9)*

   # *27 aftershocks (2+7=9)*

   # *3.6 strongest aftershock (3+6=9)*

   # *Cell phone: (interrupted) 9 letters*

- May 4, 08 Cyclone(storm) in Myanmar(Burma), Up to -## 134,000 Dead / 1,500,000 - Homeless

   # 9,000 Dead in first report

   # 900 Trapped in first report

   # 'QINGCHUAN': 9 Letters. (Main area hit)

- March 5, 2007 Earthquake in Sumatra, Indonesia:

   # 6.3 in magnitude; perfectly divided by **9**

   # Indonesia **9** letters

- Feb. 27, 2007 Largest Stock market drop in USA and worldwide since September 11, 07

   # The main trigger was a dramatic drop in China's stock market of **9** %

   # Happened on '2 . 27 . 07'. All digits added = 18 (1 + 8 = **9**)

- Jan.31, 2007 **Venezuela** government give their President power to make National decrees for 18 months

    # Venezuela **9** letters

    # 18 months $1 + 8 = 9$

    # Socialism **9** letters *(declared to be coming)*

    # Communism **9** letters (eventually)

- Jan.15, 2007 President of Iran meets with South American Countries for purported 'Anti-US Alliance' (IRAN - VENEZUELA - NICARAGUA - ECUADOR - BOLIVIA).

    # Venezuela ....**9** Letters

    # Nicaragua ... **9** Letters

    # (Iran - Ecuador - Bolivia) (**18** Letters) $1 + 8 = 9$

    # Iran, Venezuela, Nicaragua, Ecuador, Bolivia (**36** Letters) .. $3 + 6 = 9$

- Jan.1, 2007 Bulgaria & Romania join 'European Union' making up **27** countries......$2 + 7 = 9$

- Jan. 1, 2007, same as (**1** . **1** . **07**): Bulgaria & Romania join European Union.....$1 + 1 + 7 = 9$

- Jan. 1, 2007 Bulgaria & Romania: Previous **'Communist'** Countries...... **9** Letters

- Jan. 1, 2007 'European Union' believed to be the 'Revived Roman Empire" **18** letters ....$1 + 8 = 9$

- Jan. 1, 2007 New Secretary General of United Nations Chosen: *'Banki-Moon'*........**9** Letters

- Dec. 29, 2006 King of Babylon (Saddam Hussein) executed **27** years after his reign started, since 1979........$2 + 7 = 9$

Nov. 16, 2006 Earthquake 8.1 on Riptors' Scale causing tsunami $8 + 1 = 9$

- Oct. 9,2006 'Pyongyang' (9 letters) Head of State for North Korea.

- August 31, 2006 Iran Head of State defies call by most of world community to halt **nuclear weapons** development.

Mahmoud Ahmadinejad (**18** letters, perfectly divided by **9**) President of Iran.

- July 12 - Aug 14, 2006 **Hezbollah Terrorist** in Southern Lebanon kidnap two Israelite soldier without provocation. Israel responds with **bombings in Lebanon.** Hezbollah bombs Haifa in Israel and other cities. **900 dead**

    # Terrorism: (**9** letters)

    # Hezbollah: (**9** letters)

    # Nazrallah: (**9** letters) (head of Hezbollah in Lebanon)

    # Iran - Syria (**9** letters) accused of being sponsoring the attacks.

    # Mahmoud Ahmadinejad (**18** letters, perfectly divided by **9**) President of Iran, the main sponsor of Hezbollah

    # Kofi Annan (**9** letters) accuses Israel of deliberately killing UN observers

    # Seize-Fire (**9** letters)

- July 4, 2006 '**Taepodong**' (**9** letters) **North Korea's** longest range missile which can hit USA allies, South Korea, Japan, Australia etc and USA itself. It was fired but failed after 40 seconds.

- June 12, 2006 Reports that **Al Muhajer** is new leader of Al-Qaeda in Iraq.

    # **Al Muhajer** (**9**) letters

- June 7, 2006 The world's 2nd most notorious Terrorist **Al Zarqawi** killed in **Iraq.**
    # **Al Zarqawi: (9)** letters
- June 5, 2006 Islamic Militants capture Mogadishu, capital of **Somalia**, feared haven for Al-Qaeda terrorist
    # **Mogadishu (9)** letters
- May 27, 2006 Earthquake in sea and on land in Indonesia. 6,200 dead
    # Indonesia (9) letters)
    # 6.3 on Richter's scale. $6 + 3 = 9$

PROPHECY:
- Oct. 29, 08 Immigrants intimidated. They seek help from churches

PROPHECY:
- Oct. 29, 08 Piracy on the seas of the West.

PROPHECY:
- Nov. 25, 07 **'A PLOT TO BRING DOWN AMERICA'** is afoot. It involves several aspects including: Humanitarian Indictment; Energy Blockade; Nuclear Siege, Sexual Suicide; Christian Incarceration, Riches Criminalized; **POLITICAL ISOLATION**; Media Murder; **'FINANCIAL SUBSTITUTION'; LEGAL INTIMIDATION;** Ecological Criminalization; Terrorism etc.
FULFILLMENT:
    # *POLITICAL ISOLATION*
- Oct.14, 08 News Article, <u>Telegraph.co.uk</u>: 'The *Russian President Dmitry Melvedev calls for New*

Word Order to freeze out USA'…… 'President Medvedev blamed Washington's 'economic egotism' for the world's financial woes'.

FINANCIAL SUBSTITUTION'

News Article: <u>Market Talk – Business News & Forums</u> *'Europe puts $2.3 trillion, far more than US, on the line ….' - '*

'LEGAL INTIMIDATION'

- Oct.12, 08 Some experts cite 'ECONOMIC TERRORISM'. That the last 1/2 Hour before close at Wall Street stock appears deliberately done by the downward spiral (Fox News - Geraldo at Large 1 AM, Oct.12, 07 - Mike Huckabee)

- Oct. 7, 08 Retirement moneys decline by 2,000,000,000,000,000 (2 Trillion) in the USA

- September 23, 08 : $700,000,000,000 to $1,000,000,000,000 (700 Billion to 1 Trillion) being signed into law to rescue banking system but will leave the country with the weight of a $58,000,000,000,000,000 (58 Trillion) credit system burden of the world. (1Trillion is 1,000 Billion. 1 Billion is 1,000 Million). The previous Treasury Secretary says this is inadequate, quote 'chicken feed'. This will bring down the country.

PROPHECY:

- Oct. 24, 07: The **USA** will mostly be **BLAMED FOR THE PROBLEMS OF THE WORLD** including diseases. Its position in the world will be severely damaged and many will turn against it.

FULFILLMENT:

- Oct.14, 08 News Articles, <u>Telegraph.co.uk</u>: 'The *Russian President Dmitry Melvedev calls for New Word Order to freeze out USA'...... 'President Medvedev blamed Washington's 'economic egotism' for the world's financial woes'.*

PROPHECY
- Jan. 6, 2008 **'DARKNESS'** will shortly hit **NEW YORK, Brooklyn**
FULFILLMENT:
- Oct.12, 2008 ECONOMIC ABYSS, Economic Terrorism, Disarray, Catastrophe, collapse, plague, tsunami are the terms being used by the experts to explain the Wall Street Financial Disaster in New York.

PROPHECY:
- Feb. 14, 2008 **HURRY, DARKNESS COMETH** (FEAR; streets abandoned, pedestrians absent, commuting halted etc)
FULFILLMENT:
- Oct.12, 2008 ECONOMIC ABYSS, Economic Terrorism, Disarray, Catastrophe, collapse, plague, tsunami are the terms being used by the experts to explain the Wall Street Financial Disaster in New York.

PROPHECY:
- May 7, 06 The years **2007 - 2009** will be a season of **'GOD'S JUDGMENT'** on the earth.
FULFILLMENT:
- Sept. 15, 2008 Worst 'WALL STREET CRISIS' since 1929: $1,000,000,000,000 (1 trillion) needed
- 2008 'HEADS OF GOVERNMENT STEP DOWN' prematurely at record pace (Somali, England, Thailand, Japan, Nepal, Pakistan, South Africa, Israel etc)
- May 12, 08: EARTHQUAKE : in China: up to 91,000DEAD / 100,000 INJURED / 5,000,000 HOMELESS
- May 4, 08 CYCLONE : in Myanmar(Burma), Up to - 134,000 DEAD / 1,500,000 - HOMELESS
- 2007 JUDGMENT: began in the house of the Lord' with worst year in recent church history. More celebrity and non-celebrity ministers/churches fell in disgrace in 1 year than since the entire last century.

PROPHECY
- January 26, 2007 **CHRISTIANS PERSECUTED** for wrongs of false religions
FULFILLMENT:
- Oct. 12, 07 3,000 CHRISTIANS FLEE their homes in Iraq from death and persecution from Sunni Moslems
- Sept. 23, 08 Terrorists acknowledged killing 5 Babas(Hindu priest). Yet hundreds of Christian ministers and believers are being slaughtered, churches destroyed or forced to convert to Hinduism in Orissa state, India

PROPHECY:
- Mon. Oct. 6, 08 Christian churches will accept help from **pluralistic entities** and be **trapped**

PROPHECY::
- Sept. 24, 08 People **tread the highway;** They eat there; Security is broken

PROPHECY
- Sept. 30, 2005 A 'woman' will come from behind and rise up greatly in the USA
- Aug. 30, 08 Governor 'Sarah Palin' of Alaska, unknown to the national political scene, chosen for Republican Vice President nominee for Presidency of the USA.

NEW YORK

PROPHECY
- Jan. 6, 2008 **'DARKNESS'** will shortly hit **NEW YORK**, Brooklyn
FULFILLMENT:
- Oct.12, 2007 **ECONOMIC ABYSS**, Economic Terrorism, Disarray, Catastrophe, Collapse, Plague, Tsunami are the terms being used by the experts to explain the Wall Street Financial Disaster in New York.
- March 18, 08 The new Governor and his wife alleg-edly acknowledged adulterous affairs
- March 11, 2008 Governor of New York involved in prostitution. Resigns

PROPHECY:
- August 23, 08 Violent attack in New Jersey

PROPHECY
- June 20, 08 Major Shopping - Housing complex will open in Harlem. A church group has a stake in it. Large crowd attends the opening. 'Sky-rised' apartments in proximity to complex with small shops on ground floor, will be sold to the general public

PROPHECY:
- Dec. 31, 2007 *"The church is going down into a black hole, except for one little white spot, no one is listening anymore, Everyone want to have their own way, no obedience. The church is falling back"* [BLACK HOLE: Divination, Old Testament Ritualism, Symbol; Witchcraft substitutes] (by 13 year old prophetess)
FULFILLMENT:
- Jan. 2, 08 Uprising of 'Nazarite's Vow' of long-haired young men. Claims of many thousands already enlisted
- Jan. 2, 08 Christian leader agree with Diviners declaring Dec. 21, 2012, day of doom or rapture
- Jan. 2, 08 A Mezuzah sent to many households to put on their door post for protection against demons.

PROPHECY:
- Mar. 18, 07 'GOD'S REVIVAL' unfolds in Brooklyn, USA
FULFILLMENT:
- Oct. 14, 07 'GOD'S REVIVAL ARENA' opens in Brooklyn USA , 1219 Rockaway Avenue

PROPHECY
- Jan. 22, 2007 ' A FRUITFUL TREE' arises in North East USA
FULFILLMENT:
- Oct. 14, 07 'GOD'S REVIVAL ARENA' opens in Brooklyn USA , 1219 Rockaway Avenue

PROPHECY
- Oct. 22, 2006 Crime rate will increase in New York. Young people will terrorize. Gun will be used like a toy

PROPHECY
- May 21, 2006 More Flooding
FULFILMENT
- June 27, 2006 Deadly flooding in north East USA. 16 dead, 15,000 evacuated in New York; 200,000 to be evacuated in Pennsylvania.
- May 24, 2006 Flash floods in Thailand. Over 100 dead

THE WORLD

PROPHECY:
- March 22, 08 Senior Government Official steps down shortly, finances involved
FULFILLMENT:
- Sept. 08 ISRAELI PRIME MINISTER to step down amidst allegation of financial misrepresentation

PROPHECY:
- (Date lost: Re-posted Oct. 2005) Several international **ministries will be shaken.** Some will liquidate because of flirtation with:

Universalism: (Pluralism): That Jesus is not the only way but there are other ways of eternal life)- Isaiah 48:23,24

Unisexism: Men become feminine while women become masculine
FULFILLMENT:
- August 24, 08 **Leader of a healing revival in Florida,** attended by hundreds of thousands from every continent and seen on live television all over the world by tens of millions of people allegedly found in adultery and drunkenness. Begins divorce proceedings and has resigned from his ministry.

PROPHECY:
- Dec. 6, 07 Aircraft fires upon a country without provocation
FULFILLMENT:
- Aug. 15, 2008 Russian aircrafts and tanks invade Georgia without provocation
- Dec. 24, 2007 More than 50 aircrafts from Turkey are used to bomb Northern Iraq without official provocation.

PROPHECY
- Dec. 1, 07 'STORM OR BE STORMED': A storm is afoot against (1) True Christianity (2) The USA
FULFILLMENT

- Aug. 20, 08 Zondervan Publishing company among others being sued millions of dollars for Biblical versions with 'homosexuality' in some translations.

PROPHECY:
- April 4, 08 The audible words 'Cut off, pop" are heard. *'Sudden death is on the horizon'.*
FULFILLMENT:
- May 12, 08: EARTHQUAKE : in China: up to 91,000 DEAD / 100,000 INJURED / 5,000,000 HOMELESS
- May 4, 08 CYCLONE : in Myanmar(Burma), Up to - 134,000 DEAD / 1,500,000 - HOMELESS

PROPHECY:
- May 4, 08. Air warfare erupts on the earth. Connected with the Philippines. connected to a new world religious order

PROPHECY:
- May 4, 08 New World Religious order erupts on the earth in a dramatic way.

PROPHECY
- July 24, 2006 An 'Antichrist Church' is about to emerge on the earth. They will declare that Jesus is here in person. True Christian believers including clergymen will be deceived by their evidence. They will accept invitation to meet him. Some will be disappointed and seek repentance. Some will die or almost die as a result of this experience.
(Video of prophecy also available)

FULFILLMENT:
- Mar.3, 08 Oprah Winfrey allegedly begins new church. 3,000,000 join her. No belief or doctrine; No sin exists; Death is irrelevant etc, Some Christians confused.
- September 2, 2006 A man called 'De Jesus' has been declared as greater than Jesus. He is based in Miami, USA, claiming millions of followers worldwide. The cult is called 'Growing in Grace' declaring that there is no sin on the earth as 'De Jesus removed it all and has given all things to mankind.
Reported by (FOX Television Sept. 2, 2006), (CNN AC360 Sept. 28, 2006)

PROPHECY:
- Feb. 14, 2008 Hurry, darkness cometh; (fear; streets abandoned, pedestrians absent, commuting halted etc)
FULFILLMENT:
- Feb.26, 08 Major Blackout in South Florida, 750,000 to 3,000,000 homes without power

PROPHECY::
- June 7, 2006 The year Two Thousand & Seven(2007 A.D.) will be very dramatic historically. It will be the threshold for major changes on the world scene. It will be the announcement of a 'New Chapter' on the earth.
FULFILLMENT:
- 2007: Worst Year in recent church history: Majority of world renowned ministers and ministries fell because of gross sin, heresy, investigative persecution etc,

- Jan.15, 2007 President of Iran meets with South American Countries for purported 'Anti-US Alliance' (IRAN - VENEZUELA - NICARAGUA - ECUADOR - BOLIVIA).

Venezuela' ....9 Letters

Nicaragua' .... 9 Letters

Iran - Ecuador - Bolivia' (18 Letters) .. 1 + 8 = 9

Iran, Venezuela, Nicaragua, Ecuador, Bolivia (36 Letters) ..... 3 + 6 = 9

- Jan.1, 2007 Bulgaria & Romania join 'European Union' making up 27 countries........2 + 7 = 9

- Jan. 1, 2007, same as (1 . 1 . 07): Bulgaria & Romania join European Union.............1 + 1 + 7 = 9

- Jan. 1, 2007 Bulgaria & Romania: Previous 'Communist' Countries............ 9 Letters

- Jan. 1, 2007 'European Union' believed to be the 'Revived Roman Empire" 18 letters .....1 + 8 = 9

- Jan. 1, 2007 New Secretary General of United Nations Chosen: *'Banki-Moon'*..........**9** Letters

PROPHECY:

- May 15, 07 (dated) Instant Personal Credit information will be available soon in other countries where the person being evaluated does not reside.

FULFILMENT:

- March 27, 08: USA Passports will now be made and electronically encrypted outside the USA (CNN)

- August 12,2007 Starting this month in a port neighborhood and then spreading across Shenzhen, a city of 12.4 million people, residency cards fitted with powerful computer chips programmed by the same company will be issued to most citizens.

PROPHECY
- Jan. 26, 2007 I hear the word 'Sociophobic'. Despite the dramatic advance in electronic communication, normal social interaction will be dreaded.
FULFILLMENT:
- March 26, 08 Over-use of Internet communication such as e-mails etc is evidence of mental disorder (CNN)

PROPHECY:
'REVIVAL' / N.E. USA
* Scripture *Ezra 9:8 ......that our God may lighten our eyes and give us a little **reviving** in our bondage.*
- Sept. 18, 2005 <u>Kim Clement Website</u>: *"God said, hear me out. On the Northeast of this country listen to the wind, the **NE** of this country (USA) there shall be a severe **wind**. But do not concern yourself. I will remind you that this is a spiritual thing for there shall be the sound of a mighty rushing **wind** that shall come to this Nation(USA) and I will raise you up to be a **voice** to the **world again**, says the Lord of hosts"*
- July 11, 2006 <u>Tommy Bates:</u> Dominion Camp Meeting, World Harvest Church, Ohio, prophesied that he saw a map of the USA and that there is **rain of fire** coming out of the **NE.**
* Others: Similar prophecies have come about New York and the North East from Mario Murillo(USA), Jeff Beacham(Australia), Klaas Venderden(Netherlands), Tommy Tenney(USA - a song) etc.
FULFILLMENT (unfolding)
- By Oct.12, 08, A little **reviving** is breaking out in New York City. A Church with over **500 Eunuch**

Baptisms since Oct. 24, 2005. They are being **filled** with The Holy Ghost, **prophesying** on the streets, bringing in the **Harvest**. Come and experience it.

PROPHECY
- Dec.29, 2005 Known female minister in trouble with the law.
FULFILMENT:
- Dec. 2007 USA demand financial account-ability from Joyce Myers, Paula White and other mega-ministries

PROPHECY:
- Oct. 1, 2006 Pentecostal tongue talking ministries investigated
FULFILLMENT:
- Dec. 2007 Benni Hinn, Creflo Dollar, Bishop Long, Kenneth Copeland, Paula/Randy White, Joyce Myers, investigated by the Senate in the USA.

FULFILLMENT
- Oct. 6, 2006 '*A new 10 nation survey of* **_Pentecostal_** *and charismatic Christians, the fastest stream of Christianity worldwide, shows they are deeply influential over the Roman Catholic and mainstream Protestant churches and are poised to make an impact on global affairs*

 The poll released Thursday by the Washington-based Pew Forum on Religion and Public Life found that 'spirit filled' Christians, who **_speak in tongues_** *and believe in healing through prayer comprise at least 10 percent of the population of the 10 surveyed*

countries. The study also found that followers are more willing than previously thought to bring their traditional values into public debates, potentially shaping government policies in the years ahead'.
(Excerpt from Associated Press: Oct. 5, 2006)

PROPHECY;
- Dec. 6, 07 A ship runs aground deliberately

PROPHECY:
- Dec. 6, 07 Ministers of the Gospel search for the gift of prophecy.

PROPHECY
- (Date lost: Re-posted Oct.05) Several international ministries will be shaken. Some will liquidate because of flirtation with:

Universalism: (Pluralism): That Jesus is not the only way but there are other ways of eternal life)- Isaiah 48:23,24

Unisexism: Men become feminine while women become masculine (1Cor.6:5)
FULFILLMENT
- Nov. 19, 07 Bishop Earl Paulk Jr Founder of International Communion of Charismatic Churches (ICCC), accused of gross immorality (AP)
- Aug. 2007 Several worldwide television ministries shaken by marital woes exploited on worldwide media
- Nov. 2, 2006 President of 30 million strong evangelical leader forced to resign over allegations of homosexual harlotry

- Jan. 2006 Several mega-ministries in the USA under major attack. These ministries though sound in doctrine, embrace naturopathy (Naturalistic diet & healing, rejecting most meats and regular medicine).
- Dec.28, 2005 Bishop Earle Paulk Jr., Founder of International Communion of Charismatic Churches (ICCC), after repeatedly featuring avowed *universalist* Bishop Carlton Pearson.

    # Ousted as Archbishop

    # Another recent lawsuit of sexual misconduct.

- Nov.28, 2005 Bishop Carlton Pearson, avowed *universalist* and his Higher Dimensions Family Church greatly shaken

    # Ousted from International Communion of Charismatic Churches (ICCC)

    # Reported foreclosure on church building after losing 4,500 members(90%)

PROPHECY

    # July 2, 06 'Aaron is Expired, Joshua is Chosen' (It is a mistake to ignore this prophecy. Sermon available)

FULFILLMENT

- Nov. 19, 07 Bishop Earl Paulk Jr. Founder of International Communion of Charismatic Churches (ICCC), accused of gross immorality (AP)
- Aug. 2007 Several worldwide television ministries shaken by marital woes exploited on worldwide media
- Nov. 2, 2006 President of 30 million strong evangelical leader, forced to resign over allegations of homosexual harlotry

- Jan. 2006 Several mega-ministries in the USA under major attack. These ministries though sound in doctrine, embrace naturopathy (Naturalistic diet & healing, rejecting most meats and regular medicine).
- Dec.28, 2005 Bishop Earle Paulk Jr., Founder of International Communion of Charismatic Churches (ICCC), after repeatedly featuring avowed *universalist* Bishop Carlton Pearson.

   # Ousted as Archbishop

   # Another recent lawsuit of sexual misconduct.
- Nov.28, 2005 Bishop Carlton Pearson, avowed *universalist* and his Higher Dimensions Family Church greatly shaken

   # Ousted from International Communion of Charismatic Churches (ICCC)

   # Reported foreclosure on church building after losing 4,500 members(90%)
- Nov. 2, 2006 President of 30 million strong, evangelical leader forced to resign over allegations homosexual harlotry (not proven)
- October 22, 2006 Wave of teaching mainly from great servants of God that 'Jewish people today, have a different way of salvation'. Christians who believe that neither is there salvation in any other are labeled as arrogant. Meanwhile kids are featured in international news media at Pentecostal kids camps learning to preach, declaring Jesus as the only way and calling for true righteousness.

PROPHECY:
- July 9, 07 'Dung' invades the Body of Christ.
FULFILLMENT:

- August 24, 08 **Leaader of a healing revival in Florida,** attended by hundreds of thousands from every continent and seen on live television all over the world by tens of millions of people allegedly found in adultery and drunkenness. Begins divorce proceedings and has resigned from his ministry.

- Mar.3, 08 Oprah Winfrey allegedly begins new church. 3,000,000 join her. No belief or doctrine; No sin exists; Death is irrelevant etc, Some Christians confused.

April 3, 08 Famous Christian Televangelist flaunt divorce saga on 'Divorce Court' - Television.

Jan. 2, 08 Christian leader agree with Diviners declaring Dec. 21, 2012, day of doom or rapture

- Jan, 10, 2008 Preachers promote 'cursing' as long as it is in the bedroom

- Nov. 19, 07 Bishop Earl Paulk Jr Founder of International Communion of Charismatic Churches (ICCC), accused of gross immorality

- Aug. 2007 Marital woes and personal tragedies invades several worldwide ministries.

PROPHECY
- April 4, 04: Gospel television will come under attack and suffer mishaps, disappointments, attacks.
FULFILLMENT
- Nov.7, 2007 U.S. Senator announces investigation of top Televangelists: Kenneth Copeland, Bennie Hinn, Paula White, Eddie Long, Joyce Myer, Creflo Dollar. (CNN)
- Sept. 25, 07 Television in Canada reported to have stepped down after adultery.

- Aug. 2007 Marital woes in several worldwide television ministries exploited on worldwide media
- Sept.12, 2004: (1010 Wins News) The head of the largest international gospel television network accused of homosexuality, and payment of large sums of money to cover it. *(Not proven)*
- May 1, 2004: NIGERIA: Religious magazine report of recent government crackdown on certain claims of miracles by Tele-evangelist.
- April 2004, ENGLAND: BBC report of government decision to begin censorship of claims of miracles by Tele-evangelist.

PROPHECY:
- Oct. 24, 07: The USA will mostly be blamed for the problems of the world including diseases. Its position in the world will be severely damaged and many will turn against it.
FULFILLMENT :
- Nov. 1, 2007 Turkey blame USA for their problems with Kurds in Northern Iraq. Only 9% of the people have a favorable view of the USA down from 52% in year 2,000. (Christian Science Monitor 11.1.07)

PROPHECY:
- May 27, 06 Great **tragedy** looms at the open season of **mockery against Jesus Christ** and Christianity (Acts 13:41)
FULFILLMENT
- Sept. 24, 2007 **Madonna** and **Brittney Spears** who allegedly mock Jesus & Christianity believed to be **falling apart** personally and legally.

PROPHECY (Conditional)
- June 25, 04: A **strong, American-based, female, prophetic** ministry is on the verge of sinking, but can be saved if mistakes are corrected. Mistakes include: **Old Testament Rituals**, Divination Imagery, etc.
FULFILLMENT
- Aug. 25, 07 Marital violence against most **well known USA prophetess,** exploited on worldwide media

PROPHECY
- Nov. 13, 05 A great 'Servant of God' will depart shortly.
FULFILLMENT
- August 07 Dr. James Kennedy, Founder of 'Evangelism Explosion', defender of the faith.
- Aug. 07 Bishop Dr. N.G. Hyatt, Gateway Church, Florida, dead
- May 15, 07 **Rev. Jerry Falwell**, World renowned defender of the faith; President of Liberty University, dead
- March 22, 07 **Bishop G. E. Patterson,** Presiding Bishop of Church of God in Christ., USA & world-wide, dead after many

PROPHECY:
- Aug.12, 07 Flashing lights. Great tragedy lies ahead.

PROPHECY
- June 19, 07 **Surveillance** becomes more intense and personal. It will include photographs. Those on the streets overnight will be particularly targeted.
FULFILLMENT :
- Aug. 9, 07 — SHENZHEN, China, At least 20,000 police surveillance cameras are being installed along streets here in southern China and will soon be guided by sophisticated computer software from an American-financed company to recognize automatically the faces of police suspects and detect unusual activity.
- July 2007 News report of much of New York City streets to be under full photographic surveillance 24/7

PROPHECY
- July 18, 07 Spasms of natural disasters cause security officials to use force.
FULFILLMENT
- August, 07 Coal mine collapse. Experts are unsure whether it is a regular collapse or an earthquake
- August 2007 Tornado hit Brooklyn, New York City
- July, 2007 Bridge in Minnesota destroyed. More than 50 cars plunge. Some dead, some missing
- July 20, 2007 Small earthquake in San Francisco, USA

PROPHECY
- Jan. 26, 07 A child arises as a false prophet.
FULFILLMENT
- July, 2007 Human so called goddess 'Safari', from Nepal, 10 years old visits USA to promote her experience

PROPHECY
- June 19, 07 **'God's Revival'** will fall shortly upon a **'Holy Remnant'.** Covert sin will be revealed even in their households. Hypocrisy especially among ministers will result in fear and emotional disturbance. Such remnant church will be flanked by **crowds** who come in fear and awe of God. Many melted hearts will turn to Christ as the net is pulled in wisely.

PROPHECY
- June 19, 07 **'God's Revival'** unfolds in **Africa, Asia**.

PROPHECY
- May 27, 07 A developed country is **set back in civilization** from terrorist activities.
FULFILLMENT
- June 15, 2007 Gaza in Israel decimated by terrorism: 'Hamas' against 'Fatah'

PROPHECY

- Nov. 01: It is God's Providence that the barriers of **immigration** be dropped despite the terrorist activities and threats resulting from 9/11

FULFILLMENT

- May 17, 2007 Compromise reached in USA government to improve the plight of undocumented immigrants. Bill to be voted on shortly.

- May 25, 2006 Washington - Landmark legislation to secure U.S. borders and **offer millions of illegal immigrants a share** of the American dream cleared the Senate on Thursday, a rare election-year reach across party lines. *(David Espo AP Special Correspondent)*

- April 6, 2006 Law Makers agree to allow 'Undocumented Immigrants' who reside in the USA more than Five(5) years to remain. Those residing for more than two(2) years to return to their home country and return immediately as 'Temporary Workers'. Those residing less than two(2) years to return to their home country.

- March 23, 2006 USA Senator Hillary Clinton says bill to criminalize undocumented residents was 'mean-spirited' and that it would make the Good Samaritan and JESUS a criminal.

- March 17, 2006 Bill introduced by USA Senators Kennedy and McCain to legalize undocumented residents.

- Dec. 2003: Homeland security chief announces plans to legalize undocumented residents

PROPHECY
- Sept. 9, 05 Terrorist will increase their massacres to include **mass use of guns.**
FULFILLMENT
- May 8, 07 Terrorist plot to use guns to kill hundreds of soldiers at Fort Dix, USA foiled
- April 16, 07 Gunman kills 32 in the worst shooting massacre in US history
- Sept. 13 05, Terrorist use **mass use of guns** and attempted to capture cities in Russia. **85 dead**

PROPHECY
- January 18, 07 Plane hit by another plane, missile or other weapon in the USA
FULFILLMENT
- May, 07 Two planes collide in the air in the USA

PROPHECY:
- Nov. 1, 06. Known female Pentecostal Minister considers going skimpy for theatre / dance / show business.
FULFILLMENT
- May, 07 Well known, female Pentecostal minister goes skimpy for body exercise programming

PROPHECY
- April 12, 07 New material used to make more affordable homes, also used in making vehicles
FULFILLMENT
- April 24, 2007. Mineral called **kryptonite** found in Serbia.

PROPHECY:
- Mar. 27, 07 Christian church opens door to use by Cult
FULFILLMENT
- April 23, 2007 World renowned Christian University opens door to **Mormon** presidential candidate

PROPHECY
- Jan. 8, 06 Dispute between security officers of two countries or departments. One side seemingly has the edge. Guns are almost used. Attempts are made to diffuse situation.
FULFILLMENT :
- Mar. 2007 British soldiers kidnapped by Iranian soldiers, kept as hostages before being freed.
- July 26, 2006 Conflict between **Hamas** and **Fatah** after Hamas put flag on parliament building in Palestine. Stones thrown and guns fired.
- Jan. 13, 2006 Conflict between **Pakistan** and **USA** over bombing aimed at Al-Qaeda. Civil protest, Pakistan says it cannot be repeated.
- Jan. 11, 2006 **Iran** removes seals from nuclear plants in defiance of international treaties.
- Jan. 21, 2006 **Israel** says it will not be able to accept an Iranian nuclear capability.

PROPHECY
- Jan. 4, 07 The President does something **embarrassing** to himself and country
FULFILLMENT :
- September, 07 The President gaffed several times in Australia.(Calls Australia - Austria; Opec - Apec). Similar gaffes also with South Korean officials.

PROPHECY
- Jan. 18, 07 A vehicle like weapon sails into the sky to cause much carnage. Siberia - Russia - A Middle Eastern Country indicated(*Prophetess J. Hall*)

PROPHECY
- Jan. 15, 07 Small plane crash in this area
FULFILLMENT
- Jan.16, 07 WAYNE. N.J. (AP) A pilot who dies when a small plane crashed in a driveway. The single-engine Beech craft BE-36 slammed into the neighborhood and burst into flames about 7:45 PM. Monday.

PROPHECY
- May.18, 03: Islamic militancy will be punished heavily by God and marginalized.
FULFILLMENT
- Dec. 29, 06 Saddam Hussein of Iraq executed
- Dec. 27, 06 Iran Sanctioned by U.N
- Dec. 28, 06 It is discovered that Iran purportedly has limited oil resources for just a few more years.
- Dec. 23, 06 Iranian Diplomats arrested in Iraq

- June 7, 06 The world's 2nd most notorious Terrorist **Al Zarqawi killed** in Iraq
- Dec. 14, 03 **Saddam Hussein** caught in the most humiliating way. Many other Islamic terrorist caught.

PROPHECY
- Dec. 18, 06 Major digital / internet trap looms
FULFILLMENT
- Dec.24, 06 **'Safe' Web seal requires rigorous checks**:: " Beginning next month, version 7 of Microsoft Corp.'s internet Explorer browser will start **flagging** certain e-commerce and banking sites as **green** for **'safe'**. The browser will look for an extended validation certificate issued by any number of vendors......... They also will have to undergo independent auditing....additional checks.............. Many of the steps rely upon government filings..........sole proprietorship and individuals are currently barred from getting their certificates" (Associated Press)

PROPHECY
- Nov. 28, 06 Dead bodies found in unexpected place for lack of enough mortuary space.
FULFILLMENT
- Dec.1, 06 Over 1,000 people feared dead typhoon in Philippines

PROPHECY
- Nov. 25, 06 Animal disease arise
FULFILLMENT
- Nov.30, 06 Animals under captivity for recreation now amazingly causing injury and death to their

experienced handlers. A dolphin bites and pulls trainer of 12 years under water twice, lets go then attempts a repeat. Snake handler of many years now dead from a sting.
- Nov. 29, 06 Dogs, Cats, Pigs being killed in the hundreds purportedly to prevent Bird Flu

PROPHECY
- Nov. 25, 06 A vision reveals India under attack.
FULFILLMENT
- Nov. 27, 2006 US President courts Indian government official for nuclear cooperation. Within hours China does the same to India

PROPHECY
- March 30, 06 Anarchy against Christian Ministers..
FULFILLMENT
- Nov. 17, 06 Teacher in New Jersey assailed for saying too much about Heaven and Hell

PROPHECY
- Oct. 1, 06 Immigration Crackdown: Immigrants will have much difficulty doing business transactions including basic purchase and selling of goods.
FULFILLMENT
- Nov. 15, 06 Town in Texas outlaw home rentals to undocumented residents and must provide documents when accosted by officers of the law

PROPHECY
- Nov. 5, 05 South East Asian **military threat** looms.
FULFILLMENT
- Nov. 14, 06 Submarine from China surfaces, stalks USA aircraft carrier within torpedo range
- July 4, 06 **North Korea** fires 7 missiles over Japan
- April 22, 06 **Japan** in dispute with **North Korea**, send marine vessels into waters of disputed Islands

PROPHECY
- Nov. 5, 05 South East Asian **military threat** looms.
FULFILLMENT October 9, 2006 North Korea <u>**test nuclear weapon**</u> underground in defiance to South Korea, Japan and international community.
- July 4, 06 **North Korea** fires 7 missiles over Japan
- April 22, 06 **Japan** in dispute with **North Korea**, send marine vessels into waters of disputed Islands.

PROPHECY
- Oct. 1, 06 Major change in buying and selling transactions

PROPHECY
- Sept. 30, 05 A 'woman' will come from behind and rise up greatly in the USA
- Aug. 30, 08 Governor 'Sarah Palin' of Alaska, unknown to the national political scene, chosen for Republican Vice President nominee for Presidency of the USA.
FULFILLMENT
- Jan, 07 Nancy Pelosi becomes first female 'Speaker' in USA history (2nd in line of presidency)

PROPHECY
- Sept. 13, 05 Coming events will be as the world **'turned upside down'**
FULFILLMENT
- Aug. 31, 06 Iran defies call by most of world community to halt **nuclear weapons** development.
- Aug.25, 06 Iran open nuclear reactor in defiance of most of the world community
- Aug. 21, 06 Religious leader of **Iran** defies call for halt to nuclear development. Other representative call for serious **talks**
- July 12, 06 **Hezbollah Terrorist** in Southern Lebanon kidnap two Israelite soldier without provocation. Israel responds with **bombings in Lebanon.** Hezbollah bombs Haifa in Israel and other cities. **900 dead**
- June 5, 06 Islamic Militants capture Mogadishu, capital of **Somalia**, feared haven for Al-Qaeda terrorist
- May 31, 06 Taliban militants take over an entire province of **Pakistan** and establish their own form of government
May 30. 06 **'Pedophile Political Party'** formed in **Holland**: [News from Yahoo-Reuters] *(Their objective to ......"Cut the legal age for sexual relations to 12 and eventually scrap the limit altogeth er"......"allowing pornography to be broadcast on daytime television......"youth aged 16 and up should be allowed to appear in pornographic films and prostitute themselves. Sex with animals should be allowed...."everybody should be allowed to go naked in public......legalizing all soft and hard drugs....)*

197

- Jan. 26, 06 'Hamas' wins landslide election in **Palestine** (Terrorist group sworn to wipe Israel off the map). Fox Television calls it '**Political Earthquake**'. CNN calls it 'The **Earthquake Richter did not predict**'. Hamas leader vows to liberate all their land
- Jan.11, 06 **Iran** removes seals from nuclear plants in defiance of international treaties.
- Nov. 7, 05 **France Riots**. 7,000 Vehicles destroyed, many building burnt. More destruction than student riots of 1968
- Nov. 7, 05 **Indiana Tornado**, 500 houses damaged or destroyed.
- Oct. 26, 05 Iran's President calls for **Israel to be wiped off** the map *Psalms 83:3 - 5*
- Oct. 18, 05 Strongest **Hurricane** on record 'Wilma' formed in the Caribbean heading for the USA. **1 dead** in Jamaica W.I.. **11 dead** in Haiti
- Oct. 8, 05 **Earthquake** in Pakistan, India, Afghanistan. Over **80,000 dead**
- Oct. 8, 05 **Hurricane** Stan Hits Guatemala, causing deadly mudslides **1,200 dead**
- Sept. 15, 04 Iran allegedly plans to make **nuclear technology** accessible to Islamic countries.
- Sept. 19, 05 Indonesia discovers 15 cases of **Bird Flu,.6 dead**. It is 55% deadly. (In 1918 more than 50 million people died from Bird Flu which was only 6% deadly). On September 29, 2005 Dr. David Nabarro of U.N. warned that deaths could be 5 to 150 million from a new pandemic. Oct. 8, 2005 Flu Birds had flown from Asia to Russia; The flu is now found in Romania & Turkey.

- Aug. 29, 05 **Hurricanes** Katrina & Rita of Gulf Coast, of USA. **1,500 dead**

PROPHECY:
- March 18, 06 By a visionary revelation of Haggai 2
1. Universe: Cosmos, Sea & Land, will be shaken
2. Nations: will be shaken.
3. God's Remnants: will experience more provision, more glory than past outpourings.
4. Political Leaders: will be overthrown;
5. Heathen Countries: will weaken greatly.
6. Travelers: will be terrorized, airplanes and other vehicular forms coming down
7. God's Remnants: will survive and bear the seal of approval.
FULFILLMENT
- Aug.9, 06 Terrorism plot discovered to blow up 10 airplanes on their way to USA
- July 24 - Aug.14, 06 Southern Lebanon much destroyed
- July 16, 06 Earthquake and Tsunami hit **Indonesia** only days after 5000 Islamic militants march in support of Hezbollah as they kidnapped 2 Israeli soldiers and fight with Israel **600 dead**
- July 12, 06 **Hezbollah Terrorist** in Southern Lebanon kidnap two Israelite soldier without provocation. Israel responds with **bombings in Lebanon.** Hezbollah bombs Haifa in Israel and other cities. **500 dead**
- June 12, 06 Palestinian security force(Fatah) for President Abbas, **storm parliament building** of

'Hamas' in Palestine and destroyed much of the infrastructure.

- June 5, 06 Islamic Militants capture Mogadishu, capital of Somalia, feared haven for Al-Qaeda terrorist

- May 31, 06 Taliban militants take over an entire province of Pakistan and establish their own form of government

- May 27, 06 **Earthquake** in sea and on land. **6,200 dead**

(2) (unfolding)

- May 3, 06 Almost entire government of **Krygistan** ousted from power

- April 29, 06 Anarchy in **Nepal** leave King in fear of being ousted from power

- May 2, 06 Prime minister of **France** being pressured to resign

- April 4, 06 Prime Minister of **Thailand** is overthrown

- March 31, 06 Three(3) earthquakes in **Iran**. 66 dead., Several villages flattened. 120,000 left homeless

PROPHECY
- April 25, 06 **Military conflict** looms concerning **India**
FULFILLMENT
- July 11, 06 **INDIA accuses Pakistan** of supporting Islamic terrorist in India causing the train bombings

- April 29, 06 Pakistan, India's main rival test fires missiles to show military strength

PROPHECY
- June 24, 06 Trouble in **transit system**, overcrowded terminal
FULFILLMENT
- July 11, 06 Terrorists attack **Train system** in **INDIA**. **200 dead,** over 500 injured
- July 11, 06 **CHICAGO** - A **train derailed** and started a fire during the evening rush hour Tuesday, filling a subway tunnel with smoke and forcing dozens of soot-covered commuters to evacuate while critically injuring at least two, officials said.
- July 7, 06 FBI disrupts New York transportation plot. NEW YORK - Authorities disrupted a terrorist plot to attack the **train tunnels beneath the Hudson River** that carry thousands of commuters between New York and New Jersey every day, the FBI announced Friday. Law enforcement officials said the plot involved at least eight people overseas, including an alleged Al-Qaeda operative arrested in Lebanon who had sworn allegiance to Osama bin Laden (Yahoo News)
- July 3, 06 Train derailment in Spain: **41 dead**. Many wounded.

PROPHECY
- March 16, 06 A particular **world renowned servant of God** will experience enormous dip in ministry. Will receive help from smaller ministries.
FULFILLMENT
- June 12, 06 Dr. Paul Crouch and Trinity Broadcasting Network is evidently experiencing enormous challenges

PROPHECY
March 30, 06 Anarchy against Christian Believers.
FULFILLMENT
- May 21, 06 Man storms into church during Sunday service in USA kills **five(5)**
- May 8, 06 Iran legislate than non-Muslims must wear **identification badges**

PROPHECY
- May 5, 05 **More Flooding**
FULFILLMENT
- Aug. 29, 05 Hurricane Katrina in Mississippi & Louisiana,. **1,500 dead**
- Oct. 14, 05 **North East USA** flooded after 8 days of almost non-stop rain. **10 dead** or missing

PROPHECY
- April 25, 06 News media threat alert to be put in place

PROPHECY
- Nov. 5, 05 South East Asian **military threat** looms.
FULFILLMENT
- April 22, 06 **Japan** in dispute with **South Korea**, send marine vessels into waters of disputed Islands
- Jan. 26, 06 '**Hamas**' wins landslide election in Palestine (Terrorist group sworn to wipe Israel off the map). Fox Television calls it '**Political Earthquake**'. CNN calls it 'The **Earthquake Richter did not predict'.** Hamas leader vows to liberate all their land

- Jan.11, 06 **Iran** removes seals from nuclear plants in defiance of international treaties.
- Jan 1, 06 Major conflict between **Russia** and **Ukraine** oil supply and oil transit. Russia cuts off supplies. Ukraine taps lines as transit payments.
- Nov. 20, 05 Japan complains over China's accelerated **military build up**: Other triggers include dispute over undersea gas deposits, border islands, constant violation of air space etc..

PROPHECY
- July 24, 04 God has revealed the number **NINE (9)** as the **prophetic number** for the last of the last days. The interpretation of this is that the **COUNTDOWN TO THE SHOWDOWN** between good and evil has began. This number will be evident in many **future happenings**,

FULFILLMENT *:*
- March, 06 *(After years of skepticism, most of The West now believe that* **IRAN, IRAQ, NORTH KOREA (18** *letters perfectly divided by* **9**, *is an AXIS OF EVIL)*
- Jan., 06 Spacecraft begins **9** years journey to **Pluto**, the **9th** farthest planet
- Jan., 06 **Volcano** eruption in Alaska. Ask spew approximately **9** miles into the air.

PROPHECY
- Sept. 27, 05 New pages are being turned on the earth. A **New Chapter** is about to unfold on the earth. What is unknown will not prevent the dramatic

changes. They will be rapid and will have the drama of a new season or a sub-dispensation.

FULFILLMENT

- Jan. 26, 06 '**Hamas**' wins landslide election in Palestine (Terrorist group sworn to wipe Israel off the map). Fox Television calls it '**Political Earthquake**'. CNN calls it 'The **Earthquake Richter did not predict**'. Hamas leader vows to liberate all their land

- Oct. 26, 05 Iran's President calls for Israel to be **wiped off** the map

PROPHECY

- May 14, 03: The very definition if Peace, in regards to the Road Map to Peace will cause war.

FULFILLMENT

- Jan. 26, 06 '**Hamas**' wins landslide election in Palestine (Terrorist group sworn to wipe Israel off the map). Fox Television calls it '**Political Earthquake**'. CNN called it 'The **Earthquake Richter did not predict**'. Hamas leader vows to liberate all their land

- May 16, 03: Ten homicide bombers attacked downtown Morocco leaving a path of death and destruction. Two terrorist groups stood ready to claim responsibility. Their motive to hinder the progress of the proposed peace treaty between Israel and Palestine.

PROPHECY

- Sept. 6, 05 Ministers will be scrutinized and **penalized** unnecessarily by legal system

FULFILLMENT

- Jan., 06 **Pastor Rod Parsley** and World Harvest Church under investigation for allegedly endorsing political candidate
- Jan., 06 **Catholics** pounded by media for assistance to undocumented residents
- Jan., 06 Book published accusing churches of conspiring to bring the countries into a theocracy. **Pastor Rod Parsley** of World Harvest Church in Ohio, USA singled out.
- Jan., 05 **Priest** on trial in Italy to prove that Jesus lived 2000 years ago.
- Oct., 05 **Benni Hinn** Ministry under Investigation.
- Nov., 05 **California Church** under free speech investigation

'NINTH HOUR'
PROPHECY
July 24, 04 God has revealed the number **NINE (9)** as the **prophetic number** for the last of the last days. The interpretation of this is that the **COUNTDOWN TO THE SHOWDOWN** between good and evil has began. This number will be evident in many **future happenings**,
FULFILLMENT
- May 27, 06 **Earthquake** in Indonesia kills 409
    # Indonesia **9** letters
    # Yogyakarta **9** letters (one city with major damage)
- March, 06 *(After years of skepticism, most of the West now believe that **IRAN**, **IRAQ**, **NORTH KOREA** (**18** letters perfectly divided by **9**, is an AXIS OF EVIL)*

- Jan., 06 Spacecraft begins **9** years journey to **Pluto**, the **9**th farthest planet
- Jan., 06 **Volcano** eruption in Alaska. Ash spew approximately **9** miles into the air
- Oct. 15, 05 Almost continual **rain** for **8 days** in North East USA: (This is a sign from God of coming tragedy)

    # North East: **9** letter

    # New Jersey: **9** letters. Declared State of Emergency

    # Manhattan: **9** letters. Main City in North East

- Oct. 8, 05 **Earthquake** in Pakistan, India, Afghanistan. Over **80,000 dead**

    # Islamabad **9** letters

    # Jalalabad **9** letters

    # South Asia **9** letters

    # Local Time: **9** AM

    # Himalayas **9** letters

- Oct. 8, 05 Mudslide(**9** letters) in Guatemala(**9** letters). Over **1,000 dead**

- Sept. 30, 05 A battle begins for the confirmation of the **9th Justice** in the supreme court of the USA.

- Aug. 29 - Sept. 24, 05 # **Hurricane(9)** began in the **Caribbean(9)**, hit **Gulf Coast(9)** in the **Ninth Ward(9)** of New Orleans in the state of **Louisiana(9)**. Rita landed **27 days** after Katrina(Aug.29 - Sept.24) perfectly divided by **9. Katrina + Opheila + Rita** = 18 letters perfectly divided by **9**. The levees were again breached during Rita and flooding was repeated in the **Ninth Ward(9)** of New Orleans. In addition to Texas, Rita also landed again in S.W. Louisiana devastating

several communities including **Abbeville(9)**. More than **1,200** confirmed dead. many hundreds missing.
- Sept. 19, 05 **Indonesia: 9** letters. Indonesia has discovered 15 cases of **Bird Flu,**.6 deaths. It is 55% deadly. (In 1918 more than 50 million people died from Bird Flu which was only 6% deadly).
- July 7, 05 **Terrorists bombings in London**:
    # Began at **9** minutes to **9**
- July 11, 05 On the USA mainland after battering the **CARIBBEAN(9** letters**), HURRICANE(9** letters**)** 'Dennis' again landed and did the worst damage in **PENSACOLA (9** letters**)** as in 2004.
- Nov. 11, 04: **Arafat** died (**9** days) after USA ELECTIONS
- Nov. 4, 04: **USA elections:** It takes a minimum of (**270**) ELECTORAL VOTES (2+7+0 = **9**)
- Dec. 26, 04 Largest **Earthquake** in the sea cause worst, **Tsunami**: causing worst flood in history. Over 300,000 people dead.
    # Size of Earthquake: **9.** on Richter's Scale (strongest ever on record)
    #Largest Fatalities (over 200,000): **INDONESIA: 9** letters
    # Tsunami reportedly struck at around **9**: AM
- Oct. 12, 04: Surprise move by Supreme Court to contemplate removal of 10 Commandments from government buildings. (**9 Justices**)
September 2004
    # **September:** (**9** letters - only month with 9 letters)
    # **Wednesday:** (**9** letters – only day with 9 letters) 1ˢᵗ day of September 2004

#Terrorism: (9 letters) * Russian School massacre, 400 dead (half were children) * Iraq Insurgents Attack, 500 dead * Other Countries, 100 dead

Hurricane: (9 letters) * Strongest season in history * Nearly 4,000 dead * Highest reconstruction ever in history $18 Billion (1 + 8 = **9**)

* Unusual: (A) Ivan made a U-turn and returned to Florida, went west to gulf of Mexico and hit the US again in Texas. B) Jeanne followed, went out to sea after passing Bahamas, made a U-turn and hit Florida at the same spot as Francis and followed the same path.

Charley + Francis + Ivan = (18 letters) (1+8 = **9**)

Caribbean: (9 letters) where it started, mainly damaged (Hurricane means 'evil god of the Caribbean')

* Haiti: **3,000 dead**

* Pensacola: (**9** letters) worst hit by Ivan in USA
News Media (9 letters) Chaos:
Alleged political scandal

<u>News Media</u> (**9** letters)

<u>Deception</u> (**9** letters)

<u>Dan Rather</u> accused (**9** letters) - CBS *News Anchor*

<u>Mary Mapes</u> allegedly involved (**9** letters) - CBS *Producer*

<u>Tom Brokaw</u> (**9** letters) of NBC also defended him allegedly, *(now retired)*

News Memos' (**9** letters) by ABC telling journalists not to treat President Bush equally as Senator Kerry. They allegedly hoped to discredit President

bush to ensure the election of 'John Kerry' (9 letters). No involvement of the democratic party nor the candidate was proven

- Ted Coppel (**9** letters) - ABC *(to be retired shortly, unrelated to the above)*

- **Parkfield** (**9** letters), California, strongest earthquake in USA(6.0) since 1966.

- **Rejection**: (**9** letters) (September 21) Majority of the nations of the world snub the USA President at United Nations. No ovation for the first time in history.

PROPHECY
Jan., 05 Sexual pestilence will shortly come upon the earth
FULFILLMENT
- Feb. 3, 05 *YAHOO NEWS ...The disease known as **LGV** or Lymphogranulonia is caused by specific strains of **Chlamydia** and is often marked by painful, bloody rectal infection and genital ulcers. "LGV is a serious condition and its emergence in New York City reflects continuing high levels of unsafe sexual activity among men who have sex with men" Health commissioner Thomas Frieden told a news conference.. "Unprotected anal intercourse, in particular, is extremely risky in terms of the spread of LGV as well as HIV"* Now found in Netherlands, United Kingdom, San Francisco, The disease is a form of '**CHLAMYDIA**' (**9** letters).

PROPHECY
- Nov. 12, 2005 subtle embrace of **UNIVERSALISM** (Pluralism) will cause some ministries to be **greatly shaken.**
(Universalism: The doctrine that Jesus is not the only way of salvation; That other religions are alternatives. Other labels include pluralism, gospel of inclusion etc.)

Pluralism Codes:

"Jesus, God of the Christians" ....

"The Moslem god Allah is not pleased with the Shiites and Sunnis fighting against each other" ....

"Man is basically good despite his belief system" ....

"Different faiths" , *"Other Faiths"*

"God is not a Christian"

Calendars of Aztec & Inca tribes used as prophecy, (concluding that this dispensation ends 2012)

"Happy Holidays" adapted by Christian Ministries, alongside or in place of Christmas.

FULFILLMENT
- Dec.28, 05 Bishop Earle Paulk Jr., Founder of International Communion of Charismatic Churches (I.C.C.C.), after repeatedly featuring avowed universalist Bishop Carlton Pearson.

Ousted as Archbishop

Another recent lawsuit of sexual misconduct.

- Dec.28, 05 Bishop Carlton Pearson & Higher Dimensions Family Church greatly shaken

Ousted from International Communion of Charismatic churches

PROPHECY
- Aug. 31, 05 The words **'One -Two - Three'** was heard. Another **major calamity** will shock the world.
FULFILLMENT
- Oct. 8, 05 Earthquake of Pakistan, **80,000 dead**. This is number **'two'**
- Oct., 05 Hurricane Stan Hits Guatemala, causing deadly mudslides **1200 dead** This is number **'three'**

PROPHECY
- Sept. 20, 05 **More Flooding** especially in **sub-urban** setting. This will Also result from much **rain**.
FULFILLMENT
- Oct. 14, 05 **North East USA** flooded after 8 days of almost non-stop rain
- Sept. 23, 05 In rainy New Orleans, **water poured over** a patched levee, gushing into the city's hard-hit but largely empty Ninth Ward and heightening fears that Rita would flood the devastated city all over again. Water rose up to 10 feet high in some parts
- Sept. 25, 05 In **Louisiana**, several rural towns submerged 15 feet deep and devastated. **Cameron** is totally destroyed with the court house only standing.. **Creole** is 70% destroyed. **Abbeville** is devastated. **Lafayette** parish devastated. Thousands of **cattle** are reportedly dead

PROPHECY
- Sept. 23, 05 Petty road check by security forces will become a part of the events of the Hurricanes & Floods.
FULFILLMENT

- October, 05 In New Orleans, 64 year old **man severely beaten** by the police allegedly for intoxication, intimidation and resisting arrest.
- Sept. 25, 05 Arrests, curfews, road blocks are frequent. Many road checks prevent people from retuning home by road.

PROPHECY
- Aug. 31, 05 The words **'One -Two - Three'** was heard. Another **major calamity** will shock the world. FULFILLMENT Oct. 8, 05 Earthquake in Pakistan, India, Afghanistan. Over **80,000 dead**.

PROPHECY
- Jul. 23, 05 Tragedy from **the sky** / roof. People fall to the ground. Animals involved
FULFILLMENT
- Aug. 2, 05 Large plane crash land in Toronto, Canada.
- Aug. 6, 05 Plane crash land on sea near Sicily, Italy. **12 dead**
- Aug.13, 05 Plane crash in Greece, all **121 dead**
- Aug.16, 05 Plane crash in Venezuela, **161 dead**
- Aug.23, 05 Plane crash in Peru, **41 dead**
- Sep. 5, 05 Plane crash in Indonesia: **147 dead**

PROPHECY
- Sep., 04 **Flood / Earthquake** will come upon the earth (Matthew 24)
FULFILLMENT
- Dec. 26, 04 Largest **Earthquake** in the sea cause worst, **Tsunami:** causing worst flood in history. **300,000 dead**.

PROPHECY
- May 5, 05 **More Flooding**
FULFILLMENT
- Aug. 29, 05 Hurricane Katrina in Mississippi, Louisiana. **1,500 dead**

PROPHECY
- Jan. 17, 05 **Trouble in New York**
FULFILLMENT
- May 5, 05 Amateur **Bombings** at British consulate in New York City.
-July, 05 Helicopters falling out of the sky

PROPHECY
- (Date lost. Re-posted Oct. 2005) God's **'Finger of Fire'** will come upon the earth shortly.
FULFILLMENT
- Oct. 27 - Nov.10, 2005 **Fiery France Riots**

PROPHECY
- May 14, 03: The terrorist terrorizing the world today are not the main threat. They are as worms on the hook of a Fisherman, and as the fish eats the worm, they will be caught by the hook of the fisher man. The quest is to know, behind the terror plot, who is the Fisherman lying in wait for the ambush? The Fisherman is the Beast of Revelations 13, which comes in the form of a **political system**, a being & a spirit .
FULFILLMENT
- Sep. 10, 04: A new book alleges that several allies of the Unites States as well as other countries have indi-

rectly supplied arms to Iraqi insurgents. Some of these countries include Iran, France, China and Russia.

PROPHECY
- May 1, 04: The story of **David and Goliath** will prove to be a symbol and a blue print of the status quo of society and things to come
FULFILLMENT
- March 5, 05 **British Prime Minister** Tony Blair defied the desire and predictions of most of the world and made a historic win of the election
- Feb. 28, 05 **Egyptian Government** fearing the fall of dictatorship, changes constitution to permit democratic elections.
- Feb. 28, 05 Entire government of **Lebanon** liquidated 2 weeks after assassination of past Prime Minister
- Jan. 30, 05 The success of the **IRAQ ELECTION** was a blow to terrorism, the political and media Goliaths
- Dec. 26, 04: In Ukraine, a **Nigerian pastor**, Rev. Adelaja, was allegedly oppressed by political leaders

PROPHECY
- Dec., 02 An underground force being formed.
FULFILLMENT
- April, 04 Announcement of leader needed for secret police.

PROPHECY
- May 4, 03: Many buildings will be torn down.
FULFILLMENTS
- Oct.8, 05 Pakistan - Indian Earthquake. **Tens of Thousands of buildings** damaged or destroyed 80,000 dead
- Dec.26, 04 Indonesia - South Asian earthquake-Tsunami. **Hundreds of thousands of buildings** damaged and destroyed 300,000 dead
- May 9, 03: Record number of tornadoes batter the Midwest causing hundreds of millions of dollars in damage and destroying over **1,500 buildings**. Many lost their lives.
- May 12, 203: Saudi Arabia building leveled and 34 dead after terrorist bomb attack.
- May 16, 03: Over five explosions within 30 minutes rocked downtown Morocco leveling buildings and killing or injuring many.
- Dec. 26, 03: Iran: A series of record setting earth-quakes hit Iran, 35,000 dead**, destroying buildings** and homes

PROPHECY
- Aug. 22, 03: PERSECUTION
FULFILLMENTS
School girls prevented from reading their Bible on the school bus; Christ moved from Christmas carols in school; Christmas labels to be removed from schools and hospitals; Chief justice allegedly removed from protesting removal of 10 commandments; Catholic church ordered by secular court to deny their faith and to cover contraceptives in their insurance plans;

Salvation Army sued by employees of different religious persuasions; Nativity scenes yanked from schools and other public places.

PROPHECY
Entrapment
FULFILLMENT
Charities / Churches that receive funding forced to deny faith by court order mandating them to provide contraceptive insurance to employees; **Salvation Army** sued for requesting additional information from employees concerning religious background; **Boy Scout's** appeal concerning homosexual membership refused by US Supreme Court; The trapping link in all three situations above is that they receive Federal Funding for social services; Churches and many organization now trapped by contracts with 'Natural Healing Nutritionist' and organizations.

PROPHECY
Flooded Homes: (Isaiah 3:7)
FULFILLMENTS
- Aug. 27, 05 After hurricane Katrina: Louisiana - **New Orleans;** Mississippi **Tens of thousands of homes** flooded and destroyed
- 2003: More divorce in the church than in the World.
- 2003: More Christians (so called) watch porn than the world.

PROPHECY
Discarded Vessels (Psalms 36:10)

FULFILLMENTS
- Aug. 12, 04: Paul Crouch, President of TBN, abused by the secular media.
- Dec. 2002 -2003: Benny Hinn and many others abused by secular Media.
- Nov. 13, 03: Just judge discarded for trying to prevent the removal of ten commandments.

PROPHECY
Lost Ministry (Jeremiah 20:11)
FULFILLMENT
Several mega-churches in England have closed down.

PROPHECY
Endless Search (Deuteronomy 28:29, Isaiah 30:10)
FULFILLMENT
- 2002-2003 Many believers exchange spiritual growth for bodily exercise.
- 2002-2003: Several well known ministers grope for God's will for their lives. Some have found it but not completely yet they do not realize.
- 2002-2003: Several known Prophets make mistaken published prophecies.
(This page does not cancel prophets who make mistakes but believe that they sometimes try to be too specific to their peril. They may have tried to announce a 'Fingerprint' which was only a 'Footprint')

PROPHECY
Harlot Assistance (Isaiah 2:6, 1 Timothy 4:3,4)
FULFILLMENT

- 2003- New Age- Hindu- Chinese cultic healing, under the mask of "Natural Healing" invades the body of Christ at the most elite levels.

PROPHECY
Horseback Harvest
FULFILLMENT
Traditional media outreach and traditional missionary work now losing ground as technology changes at high speed. Gospel television as we know it is gradually becoming marginal.

PROPHECY
- Oct. 23, 03: Air Tragedy / Warfare
FULFILLMENT
- Nov. 2, 2003: Missiles, shoot helicopter out of the sky killing 16 American soldiers in Iraq.
- Nov. 7, 2003: Helicopter shot down in Iraq. 6 Dead
- Nov. 14, 2003: Two helicopters shot down in Iraq. 13 Dead.
- Nov. 23, 2003: Afghanistan. First civilian plane fired on and hit by shoulder missiles.

PROPHECY
- Oct. 23, 03: Germany included in occupation /war.
FULFILLMENT
- Oct. 29, 03: News report. Allegations of rival European army formed against USA army. This is lead by Germany in collaboration with France.

PROPHECY
- Oct. 22, 2003 Tragedy in the waterways & in the sea (Rev.. 7:3-4,:7 & 2 Tim 3:1)
FULFILLMENT
- Nov. 14, 03: Largest cruise ship tragedy in France. (13 Dead).
- Nov.15, 03 Ferry Tragedy in New York City (killing 10 and injuring many).

PROPHECY
- Aug. 22, 03 Political upheaval in developed countries. Hosea 10-12
- Aug. 22, 03 Sanitary problems / Surge in crime / Petroleum Shortage / Persecution (Mt. 24)
- Aug. 14, 03
  # The pulpits that disregard the many scriptures on Clarity of Gender calling it *Legalism & Spirit of Religion* will pay with an epidemic of divorce |Need hormones for sexual strength (Viagra. etc.)|.

  # All pulpits that disregard the many scripture against *Vanity & Materialism* will pay with epidemic of demonic oppression, emotional stress & fall away to a form of Godliness.

  # All pulpits that preach *workless holiness*, without personal example will descend into double mindedness & confusion.

  # *Resuscitation of Old Testament, ritual & imagery* will result in similar impact of Divination, Idolatry & Witchcraft

  # Despising of prophecy will remove the protection from advanced knowledge. Such persons will suffer the same fate of the wicked

\# The last day's impact of *wrong teaching & behavior* will be seen and felt. The fruit will show it
FULFILLMENT
- Nov., 05 Republicans call for snap vote concerning whether they should pull out of Iraq immediately, to the shock of Democrats who were not ready for it
- Nov., 05 In the USA, Democrats force secret session of congress to the shock of Republicans
- Oct., 05. Serious petroleum shortage after hurricanes in USA, causing price gouging and record profits to suppliers.
- Sept., 05 Political upheaval in Germany as a woman is elected to become head of government.

A 'Prophetic Footprint': (general prophecy) is greater than great sermons

If it is declared and published before the fulfillment, It can save millions of lives physically and spiritually. Digging up a prediction after the event only serves to promote the messenger as the benefits of **advanced warning** is absent. It is for this purpose that this page is done. No one credibly prophesied of the terrorist attacks on <u>September 11, 2001</u>, yet after the event many obscure prophecies were dug up and published. For credibility they must be posted and published by all means possible before fulfillment.

Page 2
(Archives)

Click Here first 1st Page

PROPHECY

- Jan. 19, 2001: 1st revelation of **'A Flood'** of evil: Resulting in strong believers backsliding. Others believers will be willing to defend their fall, and they will find themselves separated from the church and those who finally return will still be struggling.

Ps. 66:6 — He turned the sea into dry land & they went through the flood on foot, there did we rejoice in him.

Is. 59:19 — When the enemy shall come in like a flood, the Spirit of the Lord, shall lift up a standard against him.

March 9, 2001: Revelation of **'World Revival Movement'**

Hosea 6:2 After two days will revive us in the 3rd, he will raise us up, and we shall live in his sight.

Joel 2:28 And it shall come to pass afterward, that I will pour out my spirit: and your sons and daughters shall prophesy

Ezek. 37:10 .... and they stood upon their feet, an exceeding great army

- March 17, 2001: More revelation on 'World Revival Movement', this time concerning **'World Revival City'**

- March 18, 2001: More revelation: 'While waiting for the World Revival City to materialize, back up and start with the 'World Revival Center'. The City is not the beginning'.

- March 22, 2001: 2nd revelation of **'A Flood'** of evil is coming. Some *ministries* on their own will not be able to cross, they will need the world revival movement. They will be swept off their feet, forced to join with the harlot church to escape persecution

  # *April 2001 onward: The coming of 'A Flood' is prophesied in different denominations, churches, on television, on the streets of New York City, Overseas, Christian newspaper (Christian Chronicles) & by mail overseas.*

  # *April 8 -15, 2001: The coming of 'A Flood' is prophesied during Worlds Revival Crusade (several times), visiting ministries in attendance.*

  # *August 12 - 19, 2001: The coming of 'A Flood' is* **prophesied** *during World Revival Convention (Sermon '3rd Dimension Power') *Video / Audio Tapes Available*

  # *August 18, 2001: World Revival Movement launched at Times Square, New York City, The coming of 'A Flood' is* **prophesied** *on Times Square 'Island' *Video Tape Available*

  # *September 4, 2001: Bishop K. D. Collins and Missionary team* **departed** *for Texas to open alternative world revival base.*

  # *September 8, 2001: Harvesters in Times Square, New York City gives* **warning** *of the coming of a flood of evil and a call for mankind to repent*

September 11, 2001:

FULFILLMENT of prophetic revelation as FLOOD-GATE opens with:

- September 11, 2001 'A Flood' Gate Opens NEW YORK CITY

WORLD TRADE BOMBING in New York City

PENTAGON BOMBING in Washington

PLANE CRASH in Pennsylvania.

World Trade Center *Bombing* [9/11] NY & Washington: *3,000 dead*

Anthrax *Plague* [9/18,9/25,10/9] Florida, Washington: *Fear, injury & 4 dead*

Earthquake Tremor: NY & California: *Fear*

Plane *Crash*: [10/12] NY *265 Dead*

Economic *Recession*: NY whole country *Panic*

War begins in Afghanistan [10/14] *Many Dead*

Political *Upheaval*: Weaker Mayor [11/6] NY, Concealed Liberal

Sorcery Revival

[11/12] NY *19 New Owls allegedly released in Central*

Sorcery Revival

[11/16] *Harry Potter Release: projected movie record, $200 billion*

($200 billion initially reported lost from bombing)

[11/16] NY *Many **children** skip school to watch 'Harry Potter'*

PROPHECY
- September 16, 2001 3rd revelation of **'A Flood'**. This time SCHOOL CHILDREN are the first among those to be taken.
FULFILLMENT
- November 17, 2001: Children are **flooded with sorcery** by new box office record movie *'Harry Potter'*, a platform to promote teaching it in school, many skipped school to attend.

....

Please understand that we do not claim to operate in the office of Prophets. We however are humbled by the accuracy of the prophecies and revelations received from the Lord. These have come to us as a result of Visions, Dreams, Words of Knowledge, Words of Wisdom, Words of Counsel, Impressions, Similitudes, Godly Trends, Godly Patterns, Assayings, Realizations etc.

....

OTHER MATERIALS

BOOKS

Every Believer A Preacher
Witnessing Revolution
Wounded Witnesses

MANUALS

Marriage Mate
Gaps of Life
Christian Adornment
Revelation Outline
Ministry Manuals 1,2,3,4

PREACHING / TEACHING CD'S

(Over 1,000 topics including)
How to Overcome Temptation
How to Remain Free
How to Repair Your Mind

Power Triggers
Destiny of Diviners
How to know God's Will
Secret Charms
How to Break a Spell
How to Break a Curse
Pearls of Prophecy
Flee Fornication
Sexual Death Trap
The Evil Eye

COMMENTS

After reading "Ninth Hour", my eyes began to be opened to God's purpose for my life, His providence, prophecy, judgment and mercy.

Do you want to know God's purpose for your life? Do you have a hunger for the prophetic? Would you like to know what God is saying at this time? Are you tired of being a passive Christian?

Well, if your answer is yes! this piece of treasure has many answers. revelations and facts about the number "9" which will cause a "hair-raising" thrill.

This book will open your eyes to forces that may have long time blinded you and will cause you to delve into the God's purpose, plan and providence for you.

"Ninth Hour" will cause you to arise to become a Mighty Warrior for Jesus!

(Passive Christian turned Mighty Warrior: Shamesha Mckoy)

CONTACT INFORMATION

Harvest Army Church Int'l
2435 White Plains Rd
Bronx, New York 10467
718 – 696 – 2769
info@harvestarmy.org